FaithSearch
Discovery

Surprised by Faith
Study and Discussion Guide

PROCLAIMING THE GOSPEL WITH EVIDENCE TO ALL PEOPLES EVERYWHERE

FaithSearch International
105 Peavey Rd., STE 200, Chaska, MN 55318
Tel. (952) 401-4501 • 1-800-964-1447 • Fax. (952) 401-4504
www.faithsearch.org • info@faithsearch.org

Table of Contents

Dear Friend,

I remember wondering in my early teenage years about the existence of God, and then asking some adults how we can know whether there really is a God. The answer I received did not satisfy me then, and it still doesn't: "Don, that's just something you have to believe!"

I concluded that "faith" is merely based on tradition ("We've always believed it.") or authority ("That's what the pastor or church says."). There weren't any reasons—you have to accept God, the Bible and Jesus arbitrarily and blindly.

Since then I have discovered otherwise. Intellect and reason are not the enemies of faith. In fact, God doesn't think so either, for He invites us to "Come now, and let us reason together" (Isaiah 1:18). Christians are even commanded in the Bible to "Always be prepared to give an answer to everyone who asks you to give the reason for the hope that you have" (1 Peter 3:15, NIV).

That's what **FaithSearch** Discovery is all about. This study guide for *Surprised by Faith* (the text of **FaithSearch** Discovery) has the breadth and depth to help you—regardless of where you are in your spiritual journey—to find satisfying answers about God and faith. It will deepen your understanding, and helps to integrate the truths into your life after attending a live **FaithSearch** Discovery event. It is an excellent choice for outreach and discipleship groups at your church or office, and in your neighborhood. It will also make a stimulating and meaningful personal study.

This Discovery study guide is thorough and practical. With the Bible in one hand and *Surprised by Faith* in the other, you will make ten discoveries which are life changing. Answers to the objective questions throughout the guide are located at the end of each chapter.

The staff at **FaithSearch** International hopes this study guide will help many to discover the path to a reasonable foundation for faith. We also hope that those who already believe in Jesus Christ will find a greater confidence in their faith, and with it the ability to communicate reasons for faith in terms that make sense to others.

Once you have completed your study, we encourage you to do as we have done—pass it on!

Dr. Don Bierle
For the **FaithSearch** Team

CHAPTER 1

Why Am I Here?
Discovering that Everyone Has a Crisis of Purpose and Meaning

Getting FOCUSED

- How did I get here?
- Why am I here?
- What will happen to me after I die?

If you've wondered about these questions, you're not alone. They are familiar to most of us. In fact, our feelings of personal significance and self-worth often depend on finding satisfactory answers to these questions. But, if the finite physical world is all that exists (as some say) then there are no answers—and there is no ultimate point to our existence. This chapter will help you to understand this crisis of purpose and meaning which we all share.

Making the DISCOVERY

The text of *FaithSearch* Discovery, *Surprised by Faith* (SBF, pp. 11-18) will help you to answer the questions and make the discovery in this chapter.

Introduction

It is significant that most people in the world believe in God or a higher power. They are, by definition, religious theists. Specifically, less than 15% of the world's population is non-religious.

This is even more striking in the United States of America. National polls from every source confirm that about 96% of Americans believe in the existence of God or a higher power, while only about 3% do not. About 1% say they don't know. This number has only varied by a couple of percentage points for several decades.

Annual polls conducted by The Gallup Organization ask the public, "How important would you say religion is in your own life—very important, fairly important, or not very important?" A vast majority of over 80% have consistently said religion was either very or fairly important to them. The responses each year from 1995 to 2005 ranged as high as 88%, and never below 83% (Gallup Poll News Service, 1995-2005). Another recent survey by Princeton Research Associates (Gallup) found that 40% of Americans consider their faith in God to be the most important part of their lives. It was even greater than good health (29%) and a happy marriage (21%). Only 2% said a job that pays well was the most important thing in their life.

Is there a reason so many people in the world have a religious faith? There certainly is—and that is the focus of this first chapter: "Why Am I Here? Discovering that everyone has a crisis of purpose and meaning."

A Leader's Guide is available with answers to these questions, guidelines for leading small group interaction, and other helpful resources. It's available free by downloading it from the *FaithSearch* Web site (www.faithsearch.org). For a small fee plus postage, a printed copy can be requested from the *FaithSearch* office (952-401-4501).

Answers to the numbered, objective questions are available at the end of each chapter.

Americans' Belief in God

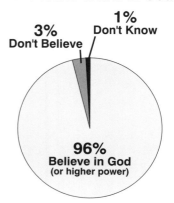

1% Don't Know

3% Don't Believe

96% Believe in God (or higher power)

There can be a confusing and negative side to religion. Some people–both believers and unbelievers–hold views of God, faith and church that are based on stereotypes and caricatures.

Read the following discussion of a few of the most common caricatures, and then answer the questions that follow.

A caricature is a description or cartoon that ridiculously distorts or exaggerates the defects of the real thing. These can be based on race, gender, or, as in this discussion, religion. Some people mistakenly stereotype the Christian faith as anti-intellectual, merely an emotion, and as a crutch for the weak (SBF, p.12).

The editors of *HIS Magazine* ("Why I'm Not a Christian," by Robert M. Kachur, February, 1986), surveyed college and university students concerning their views of Christianity. The three most frequent ways to complete the statement, "Why I am not a Christian," were: 1) Because Christians are hypocrites; 2) Because Christians are stuck-up and don't accept me for who I am; and 3) Because Christianity is too exclusive.

There are also stereotypes specific to the Christian church. This is evident when someone says: "All that churches and ministers want is my money"; or "I don't want to be part of a church because churches have too many problems, too much bickering, etc."; or "I have to give up too much to be part of a church, and I can't have any fun." While some of these caricatures may have some basis in truth and it is understandable how they started, their distortion and exaggeration do not represent most Christians and churches. They are caricatures.

Extreme negative views of religious faith are usually based on
(1) _____ (a description or cartoon that ridiculously distorts or exaggerates the defects of the real thing).

(2) True/False. An example of a negative caricature of religion and faith is that it is a crutch for the weak.

Can you relate to any of the caricatures mentioned above? Make a brief list of the positive and negative impressions and experiences you have had with religious people, faith and God. How have they affected your current attitude and life response?

In Pursuit of Purpose and Meaning

Why do so many people around the world continue to turn to faith as vitally important even though there are negative stereotypes and caricatures of God and religious faith? Part of the answer is that crises in our lives drive us to think about and look for meaning in something larger than the physical world alone. Three of these personal crises are (3) _____, _____, and a lack of ultimate _____ (SBF, p.12).

(4) True/False. "Death" is not one of the crises contributing to our human predicament.

How important is it for you to understand how the world started, why you personally exist, and what happens to you when you die? (Circle one)

Not
Important   1   2   3   4   5   6   7   8   9   10   Very
Important

Make a list of the top five most important things in your life and prioritize them from one through five. In a sentence or two state what you feel is your life's purpose.

The physical world consists of (5) _____, _____, _____ and _____ (SBF, pp.13-14). Everything in it is (6) _____, that is, it has limits and is dependent on something infinite to define or reveal its ultimate purpose. Only an eternal, absolute and infinite being (God) could reveal the answers to the questions: "How did we get here?"; "Why are we here?"; and "What will happen to us when we die?"

(7) True/False. The following are all finite: universe, air, atomic bomb, people.

Some people think and teach that nothing except the finite physical world exists. They think there is (8) _____ God, _____ supernatural, and _____ soul or spirit. If these people are right, then our suffering is meaningless, we cannot know the ultimate purpose for our life, and there is no life after death. This is the perspective reflected in the following two quotes from evolutionary texts:

> "You are an animal, and share a common heritage with earthworms…"
> (*Biology: Visualizing Life.* Holt, Rinehart and Winston, 1994).

> "Man is the result of a purposeless and natural process that did not have him in mind. He was not planned. He is a state of matter…"
> (George Gaylord Simpson, *The Meaning of Evolution.* Yale University Press, 1967).

If there is no God and if the world is all there is, then…

DEATH Wins

THE END

(9) Read Psalm 14:1 in a Bible or as provided here in the margin. Complete the missing words. "The _____ has said in his heart, 'There is no _____.'"

The Russian novelist Tolstoy was well aware of this problem. He frequently

The fool has said in his heart, "There is no God." They are corrupt, they have committed abominable deeds; There is no one who does good.

—Psalm 14:1

depicted the crisis of purpose and meaning through his characters, having them ask, "Is there any value or meaning to life that death does not destroy?" They—like many people—concluded there is none. Read Ecclesiastes 1:2; 2:11, 16-17 and 3:19-20 in the Bible or as provided below. From the viewpoint that the finite physical world is all there is, do you agree with the statements in Ecclesiastes 1:2 and 1 Corinthians 15:32b?

> *"Meaningless! Meaningless!" says the Teacher. "Utterly meaningless! Everything is meaningless."*   **—Ecclesiastes 1:2 (NIV)**

> *Yet when I surveyed all that my hands had done and what I had toiled to achieve, everything was meaningless, a chasing after the wind; nothing was gained under the sun.... Like the fool, the wise man too must die! So I hated life, because the work that is done under the sun was grievous to me. All of it is meaningless, a chasing after the wind.*   **—Ecclesiastes 2:11,16-17 (NIV)**

> *Man's fate is like that of the animals; the same fate awaits them both: As one dies, so dies the other. All have the same breath; man has no advantage over the animal. Everything is meaningless. All go to the same place; all come from dust, and to dust all return.*   **—Ecclesiastes 3:19-20 (NIV)**

> *If the dead are not raised, "Let us eat and drink, for tomorrow we die."*
> **—1 Corinthians 15:32b**

If the finite world is all there is, we make a devastating discovery.

**Discovery #1
No God? DEATH Wins**

Ah-ha!
The DISCOVERY

Death is the ultimate and final conqueror if the finite world is all there is!

Read the first four words of Genesis 1:1 in a Bible or as provided in the margin. Also read Psalm 139:13-14; Revelation 1:8, 17-18; 21:4-5; and Luke 12:6-7 below, then answer this question: What difference would it make to our first discovery if an eternal and all-powerful God exists?

In the beginning God created the heavens and the earth.
—Genesis 1:1

> *For You formed my inward parts; You wove me in my mother's womb. I will give thanks to You, for I am fearfully and wonderfully made; Wonderful are Your works, And my soul knows it very well.*   **—Psalm 139:13-14**

> *"I am the Alpha and the Omega," says the Lord God, "who is and who was and who is to come, the Almighty..." When I saw Him, I fell at His feet like a dead man. And He placed His right hand on me, saying, "Do not be afraid; I am the first and the last, and the living One; and I was dead, and behold, I am alive forevermore, and I have the keys of death and of Hades."*
> **—Revelation 1:8,17-18**

"…[A]nd He will wipe away every tear from their eyes; and there will no longer be any death; there will no longer be any mourning, or crying, or pain; the first things have passed away." And He who sits on the throne said, "Behold, I am making all things new…"   **—Revelation 21:4-5**

"Are not five sparrows sold for two cents? Yet not one of them is forgotten before God. Indeed, the very hairs of your head are all numbered. Do not fear; you are more valuable than many sparrows."   **—Luke 12:6-7**

This may help to explain why, in view of Discovery #1, so many people in the world turn to religious faith for hope.

What if someone says that they live for family? Isn't that a purpose? Isn't it enough that our life's purpose is to build a better future for our family and society? After you have read the following perspective on this, write your own brief response as if you were answering a friend.

Yes, family is a wonderful thing, and so is contributing to a better future society. Almost everyone would choose to live in a society of order, respect and freedom rather than one of chaos, destruction and fear. But that misses the point. These purposes are temporal and confined to the finite triangle (physical world) only. How is it determined which are the desirable values of a society?

Without an infinite and personal God who defines absolute values by His righteous character, the only way values can be declared to be right or wrong are by a majority (vote) or by might ("might makes right"). That means the values will change over time as people change their votes, or a political revolution occurs and values are determined by a despot. The greater question is whether you and I have any inherent worth as persons without regard to any contribution we make. If not, the significance of each individual is sacrificed for the race, i.e., you have no value except as you contribute to a future humanity in which you will never personally participate.

The Christian position is that individuals find true dignity and worth when they discover they are here by the choice of an intelligent Designer who created them for a purpose that transcends the grave. This eternal perspective gives ultimate significance to each individual, and gives the absolute context for making sense of our contribution to family and society.

[10] True/False. If the finite world is all that exists, then death is the ultimate and final conqueror.

Application and Reflection

What do you think most people in society would say if asked the question, "What is it that gives you purpose and meaning in your life?" Check this out by asking several people you know. Make a brief list of their responses. How many items on this list are the same as your top five identified earlier?

Do you think this list would be different for people facing life crises, such as terminal illness, participation in war or a natural disaster? Why?

The assumption in this chapter is that everyone needs and seeks to have ultimate purpose and meaning. But what if someone says to you that purpose and meaning are not important to them and they feel that they don't need it?

Read the following response. In view of what you learned in this chapter, how would you answer?

> A majority of people agree on the importance of knowing their life has a purpose. A poll by the Gallup organization asked, "How important to you is the belief that your life is meaningful or has a purpose?"
>
> An incredible 95% said it was very or fairly important. Only 1% said it was not important (George Gallup, Jr. and Sarah Jones, *100 Questions and Answers: Religion In America,* [Princeton: Princeton Religion Research Center, 1989], p. 12).
>
> More to the point, the important question is *not* whether someone feels a *need* for purpose and meaning. Rather they should ask, "If there *really were* ultimate purpose, wouldn't I want to know?" If you have an open mind, you would want to find out the truth—regardless of whether you feel the need for it.

Confirming the Discovery

Read the references below in a Bible, or as provided in the margin of this page. Write below how the main teaching of each relates to or confirms the discovery in this chapter.

Matthew 16:26

"For what will it profit a man if he gains the whole world and forfeits his soul? Or what will a man give in exchange for his soul?"
—**Matthew 16:26**

Genesis 1:27

God created man in His own image, in the image of God He created him; male and female He created them.
—**Genesis 1:27**

Jeremiah 29:11-13

"For I know the plans that I have for you," declares the Lord, "plans for welfare and not for calamity to give you a future and a hope. Then you will call upon Me and come and pray to Me, and I will listen to you. You will seek Me and find Me when you search for Me with all your heart."
—**Jeremiah 29:11-13**

In summary of God's Word, it is true that accumulating everything in the finite world will not equal the value of an eternal life (Matthew 16:26). But if there is an infinite and personal God who created us, everything is different. In that case, human beings bear God's image (Genesis 1:27), and are created with purpose and meaning (Jeremiah 29:11-13).

Final Thought: Review the dilemma of the "work cycle" (SBF, pp.15-16). What do you have in your life, and what have you done or are you doing in your life, that death will not sooner or later erase, so to speak? Reflect on this.

Looking Ahead

What if an infinite and personal God exists, One who created us and the physical world for an ultimate purpose? Is the existence of such a God only imagination or wishful thinking? In the next chapter, we'll discover a test for whether a real and adequate God truly exists.

Answers for the Objective Questions in this Chapter:

1. caricatures   2. True 3. death, guilt, purpose   4. False
5. non-living matter, plants, animals, people   6. finite 7. True
8. no, no, no   9. fool, God   10. True

CHAPTER 2

Proposing An Infinite Answer

Discovering the Fingerprints of a Purpose-Giving God in History

Getting FOCUSED

- Does it matter which religion I believe in?
- How can I know what God is really like?
- Believing in God is just a matter of faith, isn't it?

As discussed in chapter 1, the existence of a God who is infinite–and thus knows the answers to all the questions about life and eternity–is needed for the finite (all of us) to discover ultimate purpose. This God would also have to be a personal being with intellect, will, and emotion in order to intelligibly communicate these answers and make a relationship with Him a possibility. Yet if it's true, as some maintain, that God is invisible, intangible and elusive, how can we be certain that His existence is not just the result of our imagination? We will discover a reasonable test in this chapter that can help us to know.

Making the DISCOVERY

The text of **FaithSearch** Discovery, *Surprised by Faith* (pp. 18-26) will help you to answer the questions and make the discovery in this chapter.

Introduction

We had stated in the last chapter that most people in the world believe in God or a higher power of some kind. The pie chart in the margin and the following text reveal approximately how many religious groups there are in the world, and how the largest ones compare in size.

The top five major religions in order of their number of followers are: Christianity (2.1 billion), Islam (1.3 billion), Hinduism (900 million), no religion/secular (1.1 billion) and Chinese traditional religion (394 million). In addition, there are numerous smaller sects and identifiable groups within each religion. When these are counted separately, it is estimated there are over 10,000 religious groups in the world.

Not only is Christianity the largest of all the religions in the world, it is also growing. Some religions are in decline. It is significant that most people in the world believe in God or a higher power, i.e., are religious theists. Non-religious people and atheists are greatly outnumbered.

[1] True/False. Questions like: "How did we get here?"; "Why are we here?"; and "What is our final destiny?" are all issues of ultimate purpose and meaning.

A Leader's Guide is available with answers to these questions, guidelines for leading small group interaction, and other helpful resources. It's available free by downloading it from the **FaithSearch** Web site (www.faithsearch.org). For a small fee plus postage, a printed copy can be requested from the **FaithSearch** office (952-401-4501).

Top Five Religions

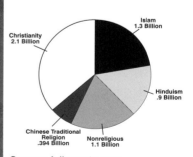

Source: Adherents.com

Read the parable written by former atheist Dr. Anthony Flew (SBF, pp. 16-17). To better understand his point, draw a triangle in the margin on this page (for our physical world) and a circle (for God) above and separate from the triangle. In his parable, Dr. Flew is challenging all these religious groups to provide objective evidence for why they think a circle exists outside their physical world. Otherwise, he maintains that their faith in God is no different from imagination or wishful longing. The Christian faith has a unique answer to Dr. Flew.

A Testable Strategy

The Christian faith says we can know that a circle (God) exists because the circle came into our triangle (world) and physically lived here for more than thirty years! The Christian God is not invisible, intangible or illusive. Draw a circle inside the triangle you placed in the margin and label it "Christian God." Label the previous circle you drew above the triangle "Other religious gods."

What was from the beginning, what we have heard, what we have seen with our eyes, what we have looked at and touched with our hands, concerning the Word of Life–and the life was manifested, and we have seen and testify and proclaim to you the eternal life, which was with the Father and was manifested to us–what we have seen and heard we proclaim to you also, so that you too may have fellowship with us; and indeed our fellowship is with the Father, and with His Son Jesus Christ.
                        —1 John 1:1-3

Read 1 John 1:1-3 in a Bible, or in the margin of this page. What is the apostle John's excitement regarding his time as a disciple of Jesus? Identify three human senses that he refers to in his relation with Jesus (SBF, p.18). What does this prove?

Two Essential Characteristics of God

You may hear someone say, "All religions are basically the same." That is an allegation often expressed by those who do not understand the clear distinctions which different religions have about God. What characteristics would God need to have to be able to solve the lack of ultimate purpose and meaning for our lives?

A God capable of *providing* ultimate purpose to the finite creation must be an (2) _____ being (SBF, p.19).

Only an *infinite* God—eternal, all-powerful and all-knowing—would know how we got here, why we are here, and what will happen to us when we die.

Circle the items in the list below that are infinite? (3)

horse	tree	universe	sun
automobile	satellite	people	electricity
atomic bomb	God	skyscraper	air

What term applies to the rest? (4)

How many infinites can there be in the universe? (5)

A God capable of *revealing* to us what the answers to ultimate purpose are must be a (6) _____ being (SBF, p.19).

Only a *personal* God ("personal" means someone with rational intellect, free will, and emotions to experience life) would be able to communicate in language so that we can truly understand ultimate purpose and meaning.

Underline the items in the list above that are personal. [7]

Read Genesis 1:27 in a Bible, or in the margin of this page. How does this Bible truth of the Christian faith make sense of your underlined answers and explain humanity's uniqueness in the universe?

God created man in His own image, in the image of God He created him; male and female He created them.
—Genesis 1:27

[8] The two essential characteristics that God must have to be able to solve the world's lack of purpose and meaning are:

a) love and justice   b) infinite and just   c) personal and infinite

d) power and wisdom   e) none of the above

Explain in your own words why it is proposed in this chapter that God must be both infinite and personal in order to explain our existence and be adequate to solve our problem of the lack of ultimate purpose and meaning. Read the discussion below for assistance.

The distinctions between the characteristics of infinite and finite, and their importance, are not always clear. They are difficult for us to grasp because everything we know, think and experience is limited or finite. We have limited power, limited knowledge; we are confined to space and restricted by time. That's why people sometimes ask, "If God made the world, then who made God?" The thought that something or someone is eternal, i.e., had no beginning and has no end is virtually impossible for us to grasp.

Likewise, it is difficult for us finite beings to comprehend a God who is eternal, all-powerful, all-knowing and outside of time and space. But unless such a God exists, the universe is an impersonal happenstance; we are each temporary cosmic orphans within that happenstance; and we have no greater significance than the short vapor of time in which we each exist. In that case, death is the final victor. As we all know, there are no moving vans behind hearses!

In the cosmic sense, we cannot know whether there is any existence or reality other than what we experience from the cradle to the grave. In other words, unless there is an infinite and personal God who created the universe and us for a purpose—and who tells us that He did it and why, and where we are headed after death—our crisis remains. That's why it's important to know whether God exists and revealed Himself to us. This scenario is what Christianity claims actually happened. This *FaithSearch* Discovery presentation and the *Surprised by Faith* text both reveal the evidence supporting that claim.

Eastern religions such as Buddhism and Hinduism think of god as
[9] _____ , but not a _____ being capable of being verified by eyewitnesses (SBF, p.20).

A God who is a personal being is capable of two things that are not possible for an impersonal force (god). They are: (10)

a) language communication   b) know all things   c) have all power

d) making a personal relationship with us possible   e) judgment

Western religions, such as those of the Greeks and Nordic peoples, think of god as (11) _____ , but not _____ (SBF, p.20).

Judaism, Islam and Christianity all claim that God is (12) _____ personal and infinite.

The Critical Difference of the Christian Claim about God

Christianity is unique from Judaism and Islam in claiming that the personal and infinite God was born of a (13) _____ 2,000 years ago (Luke 1:26-27), grew up physically as a human in a family of Palestine (Luke 2:52), had an adult ministry which included the performance of _____ (John 20:30-31), and was _____ from the dead (Matthew 28:6-7)—all testified to by hundreds of eyewitnesses (1 Corinthians 15:5-8)—whose written records are contained in the New Testament.

According to Christianity, Jesus is not just a prophet or holy man who founded a religion. He is (14) _____ incarnate (Matthew 1:23). Muslims and Jews claim to know God exists through *messages* He gave to prophets; but Christians claim to know God exists because He lived on the earth in history as the human Jesus.

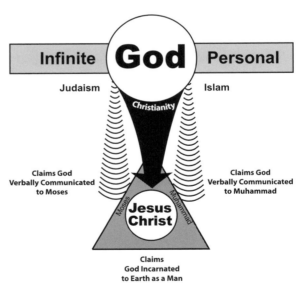

Ah-ha!
The DISCOVERY

Christianity alone claims we can know that God exists because He came to earth physically as the man Jesus Christ 2,000 years ago!

Ah-ha!

Discovery #2
God Became Flesh

Discovery #1
No God? DEATH Wins

[15] True/False. As distinct from other major religions, Christianity claims that its founder, Jesus, is not only a prophet of God (or holy man), but the infinite and personal God Himself.

Christianity is the only religion in the world that claims a God who is both infinite and personal, and whose personal presence in the physical world as a human can be [16] _____ documented (SBF, p.23).

Testing the Claim that Jesus is God

Three conditions must be met to test the claim that Jesus is God (SBF, pp.23-25).

a.   The existence of trustworthy [17] _____ records about Jesus.

b.   A [18] _____ of proof that will lead us to a reasonable verdict about the claim that Jesus is God.

c.   An [19] _____ skepticism—an objective willingness by the seeker to hear and respond to the evidence.

When someone says that they will "prove" something or test to see if it's true, it is important to know whether they mean scientific or legal proof. The following discussion explains the difference.

The scientific method of proof requires phenomena that are testable by being reproducible in a controlled environment. That is, they are repeatable. Historical events, since they occur only once, do not lend themselves to the scientific method of proof. Neither do definitions of beauty, aesthetic values, etc.

In other words, the scientific method is limited and doesn't apply to all of reality. Therefore, we cannot use the scientific method to test the claim that God came into history–that is, whether the historical Jesus was the incarnation of God. But, then, neither can we use the scientific method to prove that we went shopping yesterday or to determine who is guilty of crimes.

For these instances, we routinely accept the legal method of proof with our system of courts, judges, and juries. A case of evidence is presented which is weighed by the court. A judge or jury is persuaded beyond a reasonable doubt by the evidence, and then issues a judgment or decision about the matter being tried. This rational approach is the method of choice for weighing the historical validity of the New Testament and the Christian claim that Jesus is God. You, the readers, are the judge and jury and must come to your own point of decision regarding the evidence presented.

[20] True/False. The method chosen to evaluate the evidence for the claim that Jesus is God is the scientific method.

[21] True/False. Because we were not there, what is needed today in order to test the Christian claim that Jesus is God is a reliable eyewitness record of what He said and did.

Application and Reflection

In view of what you have learned in this chapter, how would you answer someone who said they think all religions are basically the same?

How could the discovery in this chapter make a difference in your approach to persuading others to believe that God exists? Explain.

List three reasons, intellectual and otherwise, that someone may give for not believing in God.

The fool has said in his heart, "There is no God."

—**Psalm 14:1a**

…[T]hat which is known about God is evident within them; for God made it evident to them. For since the creation of the world His invisible attributes, His eternal power and divine nature, have been clearly seen, being understood through what has been made, so that they are without excuse.

—**Romans 1:19-20**

Read Psalm 14:1a and then Romans 1:19-20 in a Bible, or in the margin of this page. What evidence has God provided for His existence so that He can declare the atheist is "without excuse" in his unbelief? Read the following discussion to help with your answer.

Can we get any clues about the existence of God from nature itself? The foundational question about the origin of the universe and of life is whether they are the result of random processes (chance) or intelligent action (design). On a very practical level we all practice this distinction every day of our lives. In a drive by the campus of the Pillsbury Company we may notice a flower arrangement growing on the grounds that looks just like the "doughboy." Would we say, "Look, those flowers happened to grow up by chance to look like the doughboy." No, we would congratulate the groundskeeper on a good job of design. Try to convince the people gazing at the four presidents' faces on the granite of Mt. Rushmore that this was the result of a chance process of wind and rain erosion!

"Writing" can be used to illustrate how we can identify design in nature. The following writing is complex: ngnylnieredcbecleuasanesnteira. But when the same letters are organized to "Design can be clearly seen in nature," they are specified, i.e., contain a message. The likelihood of getting this latter arrangement of letters by chance is virtually zero. Design by intelligence is the better explanation. Likewise, when molecular biologists find encoded specified information in the DNA (chromosomes) of living cells, would they not be justified in concluding it came about by design, i.e., it is best explained by intelligent action? The DNA blueprint that embryologically constructs the human brain and heart are so highly specified that the combined intelligence of the entire human race has never constructed a "machine" that comes even close to approximating their performance.

Therefore, the evidence of design in nature should be our first clue that there must be a Designer. To deny the existence of God is to deny the implication of the data found in the natural world. According to a 1996 survey of scientists,

40 percent said they believed in a personal God who answers prayer. To be a scientist and a theist is not a contradiction. A major movement in America today is that of design—that evidence in the natural world points to an intelligent origin. This movement is being led by Ph.D. scientists from major colleges and universities.

[22] True/False. The evidence that there is a God includes the order and design in the created universe, and the incarnation of Jesus Christ in history.

Is it possible (without contradiction) to be a New Age religion practitioner and also be a Christian? Read the following discussion as a basis for your answer.

For more information about design, creation and evolution, see the books by: Donald Bierle, *Making Sense of Creation and Evolution* (**FaithSearch** International, 2001); Phillip Johnson, *Darwin on Trial* (InterVarsity Press, 1991); and Jonathan Wells, *Icons of Evolution: Science or Myth?* (Regnery Publishing, 2000).

"New Age" is hard to define because it is often understood to include everything from groups like TM (Transcendental Meditation) and Eckankar (new age cult with international headquarters in Chanhassen, MN) to psychics and self-help groups in business or education. Generally, they all have in common an Eastern concept of God (infinite force but not a personal being). New Age thought is monistic (all is one) and pantheistic (all is god). This leads to the view that nature and god are the same. More important to us is the teaching that people must be gods because "all is god," and reincarnation (recycling of the soul through many lives) is the way that we ultimately work off our own negative karma and achieve godhood. The "self" is the final authority and is not accountable to anything else—certainly not to an absolute personal and holy God (whom New Agers don't believe exists). There is no recognition of human sin, only "mistakes." There is also no forgiveness, grace or mercy in New Age, only impersonal and unforgiving karma.

Confirming the Discovery

Read the references below in a Bible, or as provided here in the margin. Write below how the main teaching of each relates to or confirms the discovery in this chapter.

Matthew 1:23

John 1:1-3, 14, 18

John 17:5

Romans 1:19-20

"Behold, the virgin shall be with child, and shall bear a Son, and they shall call His name Immanuel," which translated means, "God with us."
—Matthew 1:23

When all things began, the Word already was. The Word dwelt with God, and what God was, the Word was. The Word, then, was with God at the beginning, and through him all things came to be… So the Word became flesh; he came to dwell among us, and we saw his glory, such glory as befits the Father's only Son, full of grace and truth… No one has ever seen God; but God's only Son, he who is nearest to the Father's heart, he has made him known.
—John 1:1-3, 14, 18 (NEB)

"And now, Father, glorify Me in your presence with the glory I had with you before the world began."
—John 17:5 (NIV)

…[W]hat may be known about God is plain to them, because God has made it plain to them. For since the creation of the world God's invisible qualities—His eternal power and divine nature—have been clearly seen, being understood from what has been made, so that men are without excuse.
—Romans 1:19-20 (NIV)

In summary of God's Word, Jesus' virgin birth was prophesied hundreds of years before it happened (Isaiah 7:14), and the name given Him would identify His true nature as God (Matthew 1:23). When the apostle John wrote in the first century, he identified Jesus as God, as the Creator of the world, and as God incarnate as man. He existed from eternity as a person, God in essence, and became the visible revelation of the invisible God the Father (John 1:1-3, 14, 18). Jesus, Himself, in His own prayer with the Father, claimed to have existed before there ever was a world, and to have existed as God (John 17:5). Finally, God has provided additional clear evidence of His existence by leaving Divine fingerprints of intelligent design throughout the creation (Romans 1:19-20). As a result, everyone, regardless of race, culture, economic status, or geographic location, can see and know for certain that He exists. (Compare Psalm 19:1-4.)

Choose one of the following to answer:

If you *do* believe in an infinite and personal God, how would you answer the question, "What difference has my belief that God exists made in my values and the way that I live my life?"

If you *do not* believe in an infinite and personal God or are uncertain, how would you answer the question, "What positive benefits have I experienced in my life that are a result of my skepticism or atheism?"

Looking Ahead

We said in this chapter that one of the conditions for testing the claim that Jesus is God is the existence of records of eyewitnesses that tell what He said and did. Do such records exist? How can we know they are trustworthy? That's what we will discover in the next chapter.

Answers:

1. True	2. infinite	3. God	4. Finite	5. One
6. personal	7. God, people	8. c	9. infinite, personal	
10. a, d	11. personal, infinite	12. both		
13. virgin, miracles, resurrected		14. God	15. True	
16. historically	17. historical	18. method	19. honest	20. False
21. True	22. True			

CHAPTER 3

Is the Bible True?

Discovering Answers to Three Questions that Demonstrate Manuscript Integrity

Getting FOCUSED

Chapter 2 discussed the need for a reliable, eyewitness account about Jesus as the incarnation of God to earth. Do the New Testament writings in the Bible concerning Jesus provide this?

Many people are unaware how the Bible arose and how it was transmitted from ancient times. As a result, they are easily influenced to question its truthfulness and are unable to answer challenges like these:

- Hasn't the Bible been changed a lot since it was written?

- Weren't the Gospels written long after the eyewitnesses of Jesus were dead, based on centuries of oral tradition?

- Didn't a church council decide which books to include in the New Testament hundreds of years after they were written?

Many people don't know what to say when someone alleges that the New Testament of the Bible contains legends, maintaining that it was written long after Jesus' death and not by eyewitnesses to the events described. They have no defense when a work associate claims that the original writings have been altered through errors in copying over the centuries.

In this chapter we will discover evidence that enables us to understand these issues and to give answers—evidence that verifies today's New Testament records to be of the highest integrity.

Making the DISCOVERY

The text of *FaithSearch* Discovery, *Surprised by Faith* (pp. 27-37) will help you to answer the questions and make the discovery in this chapter.

Introduction

Read 2 Peter 1:16 in a Bible, or in the margin of this page. What does the apostle Peter claim was his source of information about Jesus life and ministry?

Read Luke 1:1-4 in a Bible, or in the margin of this page. What does Luke claim is the source of information about Jesus that he and others had in writing their Gospels?

The New Testament writers, such as Peter, Matthew and John, all claim that they were with Jesus during His ministry—that is, they were eyewitnesses. The Gospel writer, Luke, acknowledged that other written accounts already existed when he wrote. But the facts for those accounts and his Gospel were carefully gathered from eyewitnesses of Jesus who were still alive when he wrote.

A Leader's Guide is available with answers to these questions, guidelines for leading small group interaction, and other helpful resources. It's available free by downloading it from the *FaithSearch* Web site (www.faithsearch.org). For a small fee plus postage, a printed copy can be requested from the *FaithSearch* office (952-401-4501).

We did not follow cleverly invented stories when we told you about the power and coming of our Lord Jesus Christ, but we were eyewitnesses of His majesty.
—2 Peter 1:16 (NIV)

Many have undertaken to draw up an account of the things that have been fulfilled among us, just as they were handed down to us by those who from the first were eyewitnesses and servants of the word. Therefore, since I myself have carefully investigated everything from the beginning, it seemed good also to me to write an orderly account for you, most excellent Theophilus, so that you may know the certainty of the things you have been taught.
—Luke 1:1-4 (NIV)

If the New Testament writers truly were eyewitnesses or had eyewitness sources, then their writings could be tested for truthfulness and integrity by contemporary opponents such as the Pharisees. They also could *not* contain legends since legends only arise in later generations when no one is alive who can set the record straight.

The first or original writing of any work is referred to as an (1) _____ (SBF, p.29).

(2) True/False. There are no autographs of any ancient writings (SBF, p.29).

Prior to the invention of the Guttenberg printing press in the fifteenth century, duplication or copying of publications was done by specially trained people called scribes. Their handwritten copies are called (3) _____.

Read the following, and highlight some of the ways that scholars can determine how old a manuscript is.

There are numerous ways to determine the date of a manuscript. A common indicator is the style of writing used by the copyist. There was a period of time where copying was done in all capital letters, another time when they used only small letters, and still other times when copying was done in a cursive style. A general date would be indicated by the style. The absence or degree of punctuation also indicates different time periods.

Another measurement is the writing material itself and how it was processed, whether animal skin such as vellum, or plant source like papyrus rolls and codices (pages as in a book). The technology of the development of writing materials is well known and provides another indicator of age. Further, the writing material can also be submitted to carbon-14 radiometric dating to determine the age.

Finally, artifacts like coins or ceramics that are often found with the manuscripts give an indication of the time period in which the manuscript may have been copied. The methods for determining the dates of ancient manuscripts are quite well-developed today and usually yield confident results.

To ask if a manuscript has (4) _____ is to ask if it is genuine, or true to the autograph (SBF, p.28).

(5) True/False. The time period when changes are alleged to have arisen in ancient manuscripts is when copied by hand, prior to the invention of the printing press.

The test of whether the New Testament manuscripts have been transmitted accurately from the first century to the present has to do with: (6)

      a) historical reliability   c) authorship

      b) integrity of the writings   d) none of the above

For more information on New Testament manuscripts and their age, see Norman Geisler and William Nix, *A General Introduction to the Bible* (Chicago: Moody, 1986), pp. 385-408.

Manuscript Integrity

There are three questions used to determine the integrity of ancient writings like the New Testament.

The first question is: How [7] **_____ handwritten manuscripts have been found?** (SBF, p.29)

Refer to pages 30-31 in SBF to see how the number of extant (known) handwritten manuscripts of the New Testament compares with other well-known historical writings. The number of handwritten copies discovered of other ancient writings varies from 1 to 643, with most writings having fewer than 30. In contrast, the New Testament has more than [8] _____ handwritten copies. All scholars agree that more is better!

The approximate number of ancient Greek manuscripts (the original language, not including the languages it was translated into) of portions or all of the New Testament is: [9]

a) 24,000	c) 5,664	e) 8
b) 19,000	d) 643	

The following provides understanding of another aspect of ancient manuscripts.

Are the manuscripts that have been found for ancient writings all complete?

No, many are fragments rather than the whole document. Archaeologists count every new find as another manuscript regardless of completeness. Because the manuscripts are very old they may be torn, rotted or burned. In fact, there are ancient writings for which no complete manuscripts have ever been found.

For the Gospels of the New Testament, which detail the life and ministry of Jesus, the first and early second century papyri manuscripts are all fragments. Nearly complete copies of the Gospels have been found from the late second century, for example, the Chester Beatty (P45) and Bodmer (P66, P75) papyri. Recently the Chester Beatty papyrus II (P46) containing most of the apostle Paul's complete letters has been dated in the late first century. (See the book by Comfort identified in the question on scrolls and books, on p.26).

The numbers of manuscripts cited throughout this session, whether of the New Testament or otherwise, are all counted the same. There is not one standard used for other literature and another for the New Testament.

Circle the correct answer below:

[10] There are (fewer) (about the same) (more) (far more) New Testament manuscript copies than any other ancient literature.

How does the large number of New Testament manuscripts give us greater confidence for the integrity of its text? (SBF, pp.29-30)

Integrity Question #1

Integrity Question #2

The second question used to determine the integrity of ancient writings is: How [11] _____ are these handwritten manuscripts? (SBF, p.31)

The Guttenberg printing press was not invented until the fifteenth century. Prior to that, copies had to be done by hand as indicated on the timeline below.

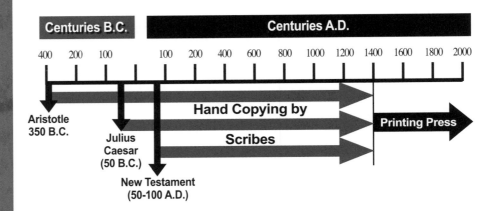

It is during the hand copying of manuscripts that additions, deletions and errors could occur. The more manuscripts that are found of a particular work, the better scholars are able to detect these changes, and more likely to restore the actual content of the original autograph by comparing the various copies. It is also true that earlier manuscripts are likely to have accumulated fewer of these changes. Most scholars agree that earlier is better!

Using the chart below, compare the span of time between the date of original authorship (represented by the quill pen) with the date of the earliest known manuscript (represented by the book) of five well-known ancient writings and the New Testament.

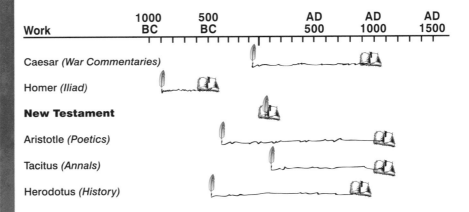

The interval between the date of authorship and the earliest known manuscript of other ancient works varies from 300 to 1,500 years. How does the New Testament compare with this? For your answer, also consider the timeline of the first two centuries A.D. below.

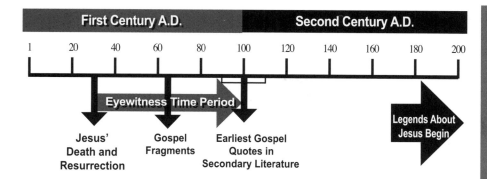

In contrast to the long time span of other ancient literature, there are full New Testament Gospels within 100 years of authorship, New Testament quotes in other writings within 30-50 years, and manuscript fragments of Matthew, Mark and Luke within 15 years of authorship.

Therefore, the Gospel manuscripts are within the [12] _____ generation of the people and events they describe. No other pre-printing press writing can make this claim.

Circle the correct answer below:

Compared to other ancient literature, the New Testament has (circle one)

[13] (far less) (less) (about the same) (more) time between the original authorship and the earliest manuscript copies.

Put an "X" in the quadrant that indicates which combination of factors gives the best support to the integrity of an ancient writing. [14]

	Many Manuscripts	**Few Manuscripts**
Eyewitness Sources		
Hearsay Sources		

Does the New Testament have this combination of factors? [15]

[16] True/False. There is a nearly continuous chain of copies of the New Testament from the first century authorship to the fifteenth century printing press (SBF, p.34).

An interesting sidelight about types of ancient manuscripts is revealed in the following discussion.

> The Old Testament and other ancient writings prior to the first century A.D. were recorded on scrolls. Beginning in the middle of the first century A.D., the material was prepared in sheets of papyrus that were folded into pages and stitched at the spine. They could also be written on both sides, similar to our custom in books today. These were referred to as codices or books (singular = codex).
>
> The earliest copy of the New Testament Gospel of Mark is a codex and so are all subsequent portions of the New Testament. In fact, the codex was unique to Christianity until the end of the second century. Not a single non-Christian codex has been found from the second century in Egypt. This resulted in Christians being referred to as the people of the "book."

For more information on New Testament manuscripts and the codex, see the excellent chapter, "Texts and Manuscripts of the New Testament" by Philip W. Comfort in *The Origin of the Bible* (Wheaton: Tyndale House, 1992), especially p. 202. For more on writing materials see chapter 19 ("Writing Materials," pp. 331-342) in Norman Geisler and William Nix, *A General Introduction to the Bible* (Chicago: Moody, 1986).

Integrity Question #3

The third question used to determine the integrity of ancient writings is: How [17] _____ **are these handwritten copies?** (SBF, p.34)

Evidence reveals that the New Testament Gospels originated from the hands of eyewitnesses to Jesus, and were copied by scribes over the centuries up to the fifteenth century printing press, *without any substantive changes in content.*

No autographs (originals) of any ancient literature have been found. The doctrine of biblical inerrancy and infallibility apply to the autographs. The following observations apply to the copies only.

According to the SBF text, the amount of distortion of the New Testament manuscripts, due to copying errors, is: [18]

    a) 25%   c) 5%

    b) 10%   d) 1/5 of 1%

The New Testament we use today is [19] _____% undistorted (not changed as to meaning).

No distortion of the New Testament text due to copying errors affects any doctrine of the Christian faith.

Distortion rate measures the number of differences between manuscripts affecting the reader's understanding of the meaning. Variation such as word order and spelling difference are ignored.

Circle the correct answer to each question below:

Compared with other ancient literature, the New Testament has [20] (less) (about the same) (more) (far more) accuracy in copying.

As a result of the evidence for the three questions used to determine the integrity of ancient writings (as discussed above), we conclude that the New Testament has [21] (less) (about the same) (more) (far more) integrity, as compared to all other ancient writings.

The New Testament has integrity because of the following evidence:

[22] True/False. It has very few manuscripts from which to work, to compare, and to compose.

(23) True/False.   It has manuscripts that date back close to the actual time of authorship.

(24) True/False.   It has more accurate copies.

As a result of our study of the evidence, we have found the New Testament to be the most reliable book of antiquity. That is our third discovery.

Ah-ha!
The DISCOVERY

The New Testament records in our Bible today are essentially unchanged from eyewitness accounts of Jesus!

In response to this discovery, skeptics often ask: How was it decided which books should be in the New Testament? Was this decided hundreds of years after they were written? The following addresses this question.

Which books should be included in the New Testament is the question of canonicity. The test of canonicity is the test of divine inspiration. Some books were regarded by the early church as **inspired** by one and the same Spirit, thereby giving them authority. These were included in the canon (authoritative list) of the New Testament.

But what is the test of inspiration, that is, how did the early church know which books were inspired? The Lord Himself established that **apostolicity** determines inspiration, that is, authorship by an apostle or men commissioned by the apostles. The following points summarize the development of the Canon.

1. Jesus Christ claimed full authority for His own words (Matthew 24:35; John 12:48), and they were received by His apostles subsequent to the resurrection as authoritative.

2. Because Jesus Christ had chosen the apostles and promised the ordaining work of the Holy Spirit for a work of revelation in them (John 14:26; 16:12-15), the apostles were conscious that they wrote as men inspired of God and claimed divine authority for their writing (1 Corinthians 2:10-13; 14:37; 2 Timothy 3:16-17; 2 Peter 1:20-21; 3:2,15-16).

3. The early church Fathers acknowledged that the apostles were far above themselves and were linked to the Old Testament prophets as to being authoritative.

4. Therefore, the twenty-seven New Testament books that arose in the last half of the first century A.D. were nearly all clearly known, reverenced, canonized, and collected well before a hundred years had passed. While it is true that fourth century church councils gave official ecclesiastical confirmation, no church decree made these twenty-seven books into authoritative Scripture. Rather, later church councils merely acknowledged and formalized existing conviction and practice concerning the New Testament canon.

Two excellent sources for more detailed clarification of this important issue are Philip Comfort, ed., *The Origin of the Bible* (Tyndale, 1992); especially see "The Canon of the New Testament," Milton Fisher, pp. 65-78; and R. Laird Harris, *Inspiration and Canonicity of the Bible* (Zondervan, 1969), pp. 199-245.

Application and Reflection

Did the information presented in this chapter surprise you? Explain your answer briefly.

How well known do you think the evidence for the integrity of the New Testament is in society today? (Check this out by doing the field test below.)

Field Test: Get a copy of the *Surprised by Faith* book and invite three friends, relatives, neighbors, or work associates to read pages 27-37. Ask them to talk with you afterwards about it. Were they familiar with this evidence for the New Testament's integrity? Did it change any of their views about the New Testament? Explain.

Write out a brief answer to someone who insists that the Gospel records in the New Testament have been changed so much over the centuries that they are not a reliable source of information about Jesus.

Confirming the Discovery

Read the references below in a Bible, or as provided here in the margin. Write below how the main teaching of each relates to or confirms the discovery made in this chapter.

John 8:31-32

John 6:63

2 Peter 1:20-21

Jesus was saying…"If you continue in My word, then you are truly disciples of Mine; and you will know the truth, and the truth will make you free."
     —John 8:31-32
(See also John 17:17.)

It is the Spirit who gives life; the flesh profits nothing; the words that I have spoken to you are spirit and are life.
     —John 6:63
(See also John 6:68.)

But know this first of all, that no prophecy of Scripture is a matter of one's own interpretation, for no prophecy was ever made by an act of human will, but men moved by the Holy Spirit spoke from God.
     —2 Peter 1:20-21

In summary of God's Word, Jesus taught that His Word (recorded in the Bible) is truth (John 8:31). To be His disciples, we are to follow His Word—and it will change our lives. He also said that His words (recorded in the Bible) are God's Word and have the power to give eternal life (John 6:63). Finally, Peter taught that those who were God's instruments to write the Bible did not write from human ability, desire or knowledge, but were inspired to record the mind of God through the guidance and power of the Holy Spirit (2 Peter 1:20-21).

Are you willing to acknowledge that the New Testament today is essentially the same as what was written in the first century by contemporaries of Jesus—and to take His words and teachings seriously in your life? If so, what changes do you need to make in your life?

Looking Ahead

Some people allege that the New Testament writings are like a novel—not historically factual. How can we determine the difference between fiction and historical truth? That will be the discovery in the next chapter.

Answers for the Objective Questions in this Lesson

1. autograph	2. True	3. manuscripts	4. integrity	5. True
6. b	7. many	8. 24,000	9. c	10. far more
11. early	12. eyewitnesses		13. far less	
14. eyewitness sources/many manuscripts			15. Yes	16. True
17. accurate	18. d	19. 99.8%	20. far more	
21. far more	22. False	23. True	24. True	

CHAPTER 4

Is the Bible True?

Discovering Archaeological Evidence that Confirms the Bible is Historically Reliable

Getting FOCUSED

The evidence we considered in chapter 3 gave us the confidence to know that the New Testament records we have today are essentially the same as when eyewitnesses wrote them shortly after the life and ministry of Jesus Christ. They were transmitted accurately for 2,000 years.

But this evidence doesn't guarantee that the people, places and events recorded there are also historically true. Are the people and places real? Did everything happen as described? We could sum up our focus in this chapter with the following questions:

- Are there many contradictions in the Bible?

- How can I know that people, places and events recorded 2,000 years ago are really true?

- What difference does it make whether the New Testament is history or not?

We will explore these questions by using an independent source of scientific evidence. The many recent discoveries of archaeology will be used for this test—evidence which verifies that today's New Testament records are historically reliable.

Making the DISCOVERY

The text of *FaithSearch* Discovery, *Surprised by Faith* (pp. 37-49) will help you to answer the questions and make the discovery in this chapter.

Introduction

Read Luke 3:1-2 in a Bible, or in the margin of this page. According to author Luke, who were the Roman emperor, the governor of Judea, and the Jewish high priest when John the Baptist began his ministry?

Would we be able to trust Luke about his record of the words and deeds of Jesus if sources outside the New Testament were to demonstrate that he is wrong about information like that in these verses?

The Evidence of Archaeology: People

What do we find in sources outside the New Testament concerning these three rulers? Read about this in the text (SBF, pp.39-40) and in the discussion below for assistance with your answer.

A Leader's Guide is available with answers to these questions, guidelines for leading small group interaction, and other helpful resources. It's available free by downloading it from the *FaithSearch* Web site (www.faithsearch.org). For a small fee plus postage, a printed copy can be requested from the *FaithSearch* office (952-401-4501).

Now in the fifteenth year of the reign of Tiberius Caesar, when Pontius Pilate was governor of Judea, and Herod was tetrarch of Galilee, and his brother Philip was tetrarch of the region of Ituraea and Trachonitis, and Lysanias was tetrarch of Abilene, in the high priesthood of Annas and Caiaphas, the word of God came to John, the son of Zacharias, in the wilderness.
—Luke 3:1-2

For a recent article on bone boxes (including that of Caiaphas) see Steven Fine, "Why Bone Boxes?" *Biblical Archaeology Review*, 27 (Sept./Oct. 2001), pp. 38-44.

How can we know that Joseph Caiaphas, whose name is engraved on the bone box found by archaeologists in Jerusalem, is the same Caiaphas mentioned in the Bible?

The Caiaphas family has been confirmed from both Christian and Jewish sources, including several rabbinic works, as a prominent family in first century Israel. The Caiaphas ossuary box (shown in the margin) was found in a limestone cave together with ossuaries for a son (Simon, son of Joseph) and two daughters (Miriam and Salome).

The Jewish historian, Flavius Josephus, writing at the end of the first century in his *Antiquities of the Jews*, recounts the Sanhedrin trial of Jesus. He states that the high priest who presided over the Sanhedrin at that time was Joseph Caiaphas.

The custom of secondary burial in limestone ossuaries was practiced by the Jews during the century preceding the destruction of the Second Temple by the Romans in A.D. 70. Thus, the evidence is conclusive that the Caiaphas high priest referred to in the New Testament Gospels is the same person found in the Jerusalem ossuary.

[1] True/False. According to the archaeological evidence presented in the SBF text, the names of Pontius Pilate, Tiberius and Caiaphas are legendary creations of the Gospel writers rather than real people in history.

New Testament references to [2] _____ are historically real; for example, Jesus' brother James (SBF, p.38), governor Pontius Pilate and high priest Caiaphas.

The Evidence of Archaeology: Places

Many places, people and events referred to in the New Testament have been confirmed as historical by archaeological discoveries. A few examples are identified in the chart below.

Site or Artifact	Location	Related Scripture
Roman census (SBF, p.40)	Bethlehem	Luke 2:1-3
Tomb of Caiaphas (SBF, p.39)	Jerusalem	Luke 3:2
Pool of Siloam (SBF, p.42)	Jerusalem	John 9:7
Peter's home (SBF, p.58)	Capernaum	Matthew 8:14
"Jesus boat" (SBF, p.61)	Sea of Galilee	Luke 5:2
Pool of Bethesda (SBF, p.42)	Jerusalem	John 5:2
Gergesa (SBF, p.42)	Sea of Galilee	Luke 8:26
Silversmith shops	Ephesus	Acts 19:24
Politarchs (City officials, SBF, p.43)	Thessalonica	Acts 17:6
Meat market inscription	Corinth	1 Corinthians 10:25
Marketplace	Philippi	Acts 16:12
Sodom & Gomorrah	Syria	Genesis 19; Matthew 11:23-24
Hittites	Turkey	Joshua 1:4

Match the place below with the Biblical reference by placing the letter of the reference on the blank:

(3) _____ Pool of Siloam   a. Acts 19:24
(4) _____ Mount of Olives   b. John 9:7
(5) _____ Capernaum and synagogue   c. Luke 4:31-33
(6) _____ Silversmith shops   d. John 5:2
(7) _____ Pool of Bethesda   e. Luke 19:1
(8) _____ Jericho   f. Luke 22:39

Read Luke 7:1-5 in a Bible, or in the margin of this page. Refer to SBF, pp.41-42, for the evidence from archaeology that confirms the existence of a Jewish synagogue in Capernaum in the first century. According to Luke, who built the synagogue there? (9) _____

Read John 9:7 in a Bible, or in the margin of this page. Refer to SBF, p.42, for confirmation that the Pool of Siloam has been found thereby supporting this biblical reference as historically reliable.

(10)True/False.   New Testament references to places are historically real; for example, the Capernaum synagogue (SBF, p.41), Peter's home (SBF, p.58), and the Pool of Siloam (SBF, p.42).

The Evidence of Archaeology: Events

Throughout much of the twentieth century, biblical critics questioned the historical truthfulness of the crucifixion of Jesus. They did not believe that nails were available or used for crucifixion in Israel at the time of Jesus. Archaeological evidence has now removed these objections.

Read Luke 24:39 and John 20:20 in a Bible, or in the margin of this page. Why would Jesus show the disciples His hands, feet and side?

Read John 20:25 and 27-28 in a Bible, or in the margin of this page. What was the test that Jesus' disciple, Thomas, demanded in order to believe that He was resurrected?

What does Thomas' final response prove?

Read about the first century crucifixion victim found in 1968 by archaeologists in Jerusalem (SBF, pp.42-43), and then answer the following question:

When He had completed all His discourse in the hearing of the people, He went to Capernaum. And a centurion's slave, who was highly regarded by him, was sick and about to die. When he heard about Jesus, he sent some Jewish elders asking Him to come and save the life of his slave. When they came to Jesus, they earnestly implored Him, saying, "He is worthy for You to grant this to him; for he loves our nation and it was he who built us our synagogue."
—Luke 7:1-5

…and said to him, "Go, wash in the pool of Siloam" (which is translated, Sent). So he went away and washed, and came back seeing.
—John 9:7

"See My hands and My feet, that it is I Myself; touch Me and see, for a spirit does not have flesh and bones as you see that I have."
—Luke 24:39

And when He had said this, He showed them both His hands and His side. The disciples then rejoiced when they saw the Lord.
—John 20:20

So the other disciples were saying to him, "We have seen the Lord!" But he said to them, "Unless I see in His hands the imprint of the nails, and put my finger into the place of the nails, and put my hand into His side, I will not believe."

Then He said to Thomas, "Reach here with your finger, and see My hands; and reach here your hand and put it into My side; and do not be unbelieving, but believing."

Thomas answered and said to Him, "My Lord and my God!"
—John 20:25,27-28

[11]True/False.   The use of nails for crucifixion in first century Jerusalem, as described for Jesus' crucifixion in the Gospels, has been verified by archaeology.

Archaeology has demonstrated that New Testament references to events are historically real; for example, the Roman [12] _____ decree of Caesar Augustus recorded in Luke 2:1-2 (SBF, pp.40-41). But archaeology does have some limitations. The following discussion illustrates that archaeology cannot answer every question.

The role of modern archaeology since its inception in the middle of the nineteenth century has been very instrumental in lending credibility to the history of the Bible. But it can't tell us everything. What limitation does archaeology have as it relates to the Bible?

Archaeology cannot restore the spiritual significance of an event. The hand of God (intervention) is a faith position—reasonable and historically possible—but not the conclusion of an archaeological observation, per se.

For example, archaeology can determine that the walls of Jericho collapsed outward, but it cannot know whether God acted to push them out. Archaeology can confirm the historical destruction of Jericho and the time, but it cannot say whether the city's destruction was a judgment of God on the Caananites. Likewise, archaeology cannot answer the questions whether God gave the Israelites instructions on how to conquer Jericho, or whether Sodom and Gomorrah's destruction was the result of God's act of judgment. (On Jericho, see Joshua 6 and Hebrews 11:30; for Sodom and Gomorrah, see Genesis 19 and Luke 17:28-30.)

[13]True/False. The New Testament is considered historically reliable when you consider the external evidence. Archaeology is one such kind of evidence.

Testimony of Scholars

Match the statement about the New Testament below with the scholar who said it (SBF, pp.43-45).

[14] _____ Luke is "a historian of the first rank."

[15] _____ "The Bible can do nothing but gain from an increase in knowledge."

[16] _____ Archaeological discoveries have "brought increased recognition to the value of the Bible as a source of history."

a. William Albright   b. Frederic Kenyon   c. William Ramsay

The many testimonies of [17] _____ also affirm the historical accuracy of the New Testament.

Early Date of Writing

Explain briefly why it would be easier for you to detect the fabrication of an event to which you were an eyewitness, compared to one which you had heard from your grandmother, which in turn had occurred in her mother's lifetime.

Consider this quote from *Surprised by Faith* (p. 46): "Christian teaching about Jesus' life, death and resurrection originated and was accepted in Jerusalem, where the people [as eyewitnesses] were in the best position to know whether or not it was true, and where accepting it could cost them dearly." In view of your answer to the question immediately above, explain briefly how this quote weakens the allegation by some people that the New Testament accounts of Jesus' life are fabricated legends.

Legendary accounts about events and people have never been shown to originate and be accepted as historically true within the same generation in which the events occurred or the people lived. Since the New Testament Gospels have been shown to be eyewitness accounts, it is virtually certain that they are not legends. This is especially true when the records were tested on eyewitness opponents of early Christianity who lived in the same area and were in the best position to know whether or not they were true. This is the same conclusion of A.N. Sherwin-White, an internationally recognized historian:

> ....[F]or these stories to be legends, the rate of legendary accumulation would have to be 'unbelievable'; more generations are needed... [E]ven the span of two generations is too short to allow legendary tendencies to wipe out the hard core of historical fact (A.N. Sherwin-White, *Roman Society and Roman Law in the New Testament*, p.190).

The discovery of [18] _____ century manuscripts of the New Testament also supports the historical reliability of the New Testament.

Based on all of the information presented in this chapter, identify in your own words three areas in which historical and scientific evidence has strengthened confidence in the historical reliability of the New Testament record.

The evidence presented in this chapter leads us to a fourth important discovery.

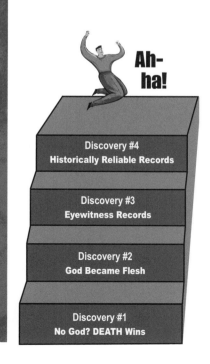

Ah-ha!
The DISCOVERY

Archaeological discoveries have confirmed that the New Testament writings are historically reliable!

Some people agree with this fourth discovery, but still wonder about the alleged errors and contradictions in the Gospel accounts of Jesus. How can the Bible be trusted if these allegations are valid? The following discussion gives some perspective on this matter.

① VARIATIONS
      US
② CONTRADICTIONS
      US
③ FALSEHOODS

The honest skeptic will find help in this area by consulting one or more of the following: Norman Geisler and Thomas Howe, *When Critics Ask: A Popular Handbook of Bible Difficulties* (Victor Books, 1992); Gleason L. Archer, *New International Encyclopedia of Bible Difficulties* (Zondervan Publishing House, 2001); John W. Haley, *Alleged Discrepancies of the Bible,* (Whitaker House, 2003).

If a person is inclined to "want" an error to be found in the Gospel accounts, in order to justify their unbelief, they will find no shortage of opportunities to claim such exist. In this case they are usually *not interested* in hearing logical and reasonable explanations that could resolve the difficulty. Their position is, "Don't confuse me with the facts, my mind is made up!"

There are *apparent* difficulties in variations of the eyewitness accounts. But the writers of the New Testament, with their solid record of integrity and historical reliability, deserve enough respect to give them the benefit of the doubt when information is lacking to resolve every difficulty. This is especially true in view of the fact that many apparent contradictions which were claimed by critics 100 years ago, have since been resolved or eliminated by new understanding as a result of the discovery of external evidence, such as ancient manuscripts and archaeological artifacts.

Furthermore, nearly all of the alleged "errors" that have been identified by people are not errors at all. Most are selective reporting that are not logically in contradiction. For example, how many angels were in Jesus' tomb when the women first visited it on Easter morning? Matthew and Mark refer to one (Matthew 28:2-5; Mark 16:4-5), Luke to two (Luke 24:4) and John doesn't record that incident at all. But Matthew and Mark don't say, "There were not two." There could have been two.

To be an actual contradiction one writer must say, "Black, not white," and the other, "White, not black." Whole books have been written to examine these issues in the Bible and to offer logical and reasonable explanations. (See margin for titles.)

Application and Reflection

What evidence in this chapter, if any, was unexpected or came as a surprise to you?

In what ways has this chapter changed your view of the New Testament or strengthened your faith?

Based on what you have learned in this chapter, write out a brief answer to someone who asks, "Why do you believe that the New Testament writings about Jesus can be trusted?" (This will be helpful preparation for discussion with those who do the field test in the next question.)

But in your hearts set apart Christ as Lord. Always be prepared to give an answer to everyone who asks you to give the reason for the hope that you have. But do this with gentleness and respect...
     —1 Peter 3:15 (NIV)

According to 1 Peter 3:15, what command is given to the believer who is asked a question like this?

How does it say you should do it?

Field Test: Invite three skeptical or unbelieving friends, relatives, neighbors, or work associates to read pages 37-48 in *Surprised by Faith*. Tell them you are interested in their perspective. Arrange a time to meet and discuss the subject with them.

Were they aware of the archaeological evidence for the New Testament that was presented there?

Did it seem that this evidence made them more open to the Christian faith?

There is an increase of religious diversity in our society, and with it, diverging truth claims for various sacred texts. How do other religious writings compare to the New Testament's integrity and historical reliability? Read the following discussion comparing a selection of sacred texts. Highlight points that are in contrast with the evidence for the New Testament.

Eastern religions like Hinduism and Buddhism do not put the same emphasis on textual studies that we do in the West. Truth for them is not measured so much by a historically reliable record (or person) as it is in religious authority or experience. They feel that if it "works" to create a spiritual experience or if it has a long-standing tradition, then it is valid. The history of their sacred books as measured by early, numerous and accurate texts is not important. As a result, they are not concerned by having few texts to work with if asked to document authorship, integrity or historical reliability.

On the other hand, Muslims claim that their Qur'an has more integrity and is more reliable than the New Testament. They point out that they have only one version of their holy book and everyone's copy is identical to what God dictated to Muhammad in the seventh century A.D.

But that is not the complete story. They either don't know or don't tell that within twenty years of Muhammad's death the Qur'an had suffered from such a large collection of variants that it necessitated the Orthmanic revision. "In fact, there are still seven ways to read the text (vocalization and punctuation), all based on Orthman's recension" (Norman L. Geisler and William E. Nix, *A General Introduction to the Bible* [Moody Press, 1986], p.475). There is also an intolerance among Muslims toward scholarly textual criticism. The Qur'an must not be subjected to any form of criticism—any questioning of it is considered heresy (Stephen Neill, *Christian Faith & Other Faiths* [InterVarsity Press, 1984], pp.57-90). Until recently, all early variant Qur'an texts had been lost or intentionally destroyed so that there was no way to determine how the current Qur'an compares to the original text (which has never been found).

A large cache of early manuscripts has recently been found but not yet published. Early indications are that, as would be expected, there are textual variations. If this is true, then the current Qur'an is not the only version (as Muslims allege) and it must be subjected to the same textual studies as the New Testament or any other ancient document. Until that is done, there is no way to determine its integrity and historical reliability based on textual and external evidence.

Finally, the Mormons claim that their holy book, written by Joseph Smith, the Book of Mormon, has integrity and is reliable. They point out that this is a record of Jesus when he visited the Americas. There are similarities to the New Testament Gospels, for example, the names of people, cities, and geographic features like rivers and mountains. But unlike the biblical Gospels, when you try to find any external evidence for them in the archaeology and history of the Americas—they are nowhere to be found! Rather than being supported by the external evidence—the Book of Mormon is refuted by it. It is more consistent with the evidence to classify this book as mythology.

No matter which religions or religious literature you compare, the New Testament emerges as unique in its depth of evidence for integrity and historical reliability.

Confirming the Discovery

Read the references below in a Bible, or as provided here in the margin. Write below how the main teaching of each relates to or confirms the discovery made in this chapter.

1 John 1:1-2

2 Peter 3:2

John 12:48

2 Timothy 3:14-15

What was from the beginning, what we have heard, what we have looked at and touched with our hands, concerning the Word of Life—and the life was manifested, and we have seen and testify and proclaim to you the eternal life, which was with the Father and was manifested to us—
—1 John 1:1-2

…that you should remember the words spoken beforehand by the holy prophets and the commandment of the Lord and Savior spoken by your apostles. (Compare 2 Peter 3:15-16.)
—2 Peter 3:2

"He who rejects Me, and does not receive My sayings, has one who judges him; the word I spoke is what will judge him at the last day." (Compare 1 Thessalonians 2:13.)
—John 12:48

You, however, continue in the things you have learned and become convinced of, knowing from whom you have learned them, and that from childhood you have known the sacred writings which are able to give you the wisdom that leads to salvation through faith which is in Christ Jesus. (Compare 2 Timothy 3:16-17.)
—2 Timothy 3:14-15

In summary of God's Word, the apostle John testified that he was writing about a Jesus whom he actually heard speak, actually saw, and actually embraced in his arms—a real man of history! Yet Jesus existed from eternity and in Him is eternal life (1 John 1:1-2). Just like the holy prophets spoke and recorded the Old Testament truth of God, so the apostles of Jesus spoke and recorded the truth recorded as the New Testament. Both are authoritative Scripture (2 Peter 3:2). Jesus fully expected that His words recorded in the New Testament would be preserved intact throughout the centuries and that all people will be held accountable to them (John 12:48). Paul admonishes Timothy to stay faithful to the historic sacred writings of the Old Testament and the New Testament truths he was taught. They will continue to be the power of God for salvation (2 Timothy 3:14-15).

Why is *FaithSearch* Discovery so concerned about demonstrating the reliability of the New Testament? Asked another way, why is it so important for the argument of God's existence that the New Testament is a trustworthy, first-century, historical record? Read the quote below from the book, *Understanding the Times,* for additional assistance in formulating your written answer.

Excerpt from: David A. Noebel, *Understanding the Times* (Harvest House Publishers, 1991) pp.764-766.

> Christians believe the basis for their entire worldview appeared in human history in the form of Jesus Christ almost two thousand years ago. While "Christ died for our sins" is solid orthodox Christian theology, "Christ died" is history. In Christianity, doctrine is based on historical events. To shatter Christian doctrine and the Christian worldview, one need only shatter its historical underpinnings… The historical Bible (the written Word) and Jesus Christ (the living Word) are the two cornerstones of the Christian worldview. If the Bible is not history, or if Jesus Christ is not "God with us" (Matthew 1:25), Christianity crumbles. Therefore, Christians need to invest a great deal of time and effort defending both foundation stones… Thus for the Christian, history is supremely important. Either Christ is a historical figure and the Bible is a historical document that describes God's communication with man and records events in the life of Christ, or the Christian faith is bankrupt. As St. Paul says, if Christ is not raised from the dead (historically) then our faith is in vain (1 Corinthians 15:14).

Knowing that the New Testament is historically reliable is the essential condition for testing the claim that [19] _____ is God.

Looking Ahead

Evidence has been given to support the claim that the people of the New Testament, including Jesus, actually lived as the New Testament says they did. But that does not necessarily prove that Jesus was the incarnation of God to earth. Some people claim that Jesus was simply a great moral teacher or a secondary deity. The evidence considered in the next chapter will help you decide whether Jesus is God as Christians claim.

Answers for the objective questions in this chapter:

1. False	2. people	3. b	4. False	5. c
6. a	7. d	8. e	9. The centurion	10. True
11. True	12. census	13. True	14. c	15. b
16. a	17. scholars	18. first	19. Jesus	

CHAPTER 5

Is Jesus Really God?

Discovering that He Often Said So!

Getting FOCUSED

- Did Jesus ever claim to be God?
- How can Jesus be a man on earth and God of the universe at the same time?
- What makes Jesus different from others who have claimed deity?

A Leader's Guide is available with answers to these questions, guidelines for leading small group interaction, and other helpful resources. It's available free by downloading it from the *FaithSearch* Web site (www.faithsearch.org). For a small fee plus postage, a printed copy can be requested from the *FaithSearch* office (952-401-4501).

A unique element of the Christian faith is the teaching that Jesus Christ is the incarnation to earth of the infinite and personal God. Was this only the idea of the later church, or did Jesus, Himself, ever make such a claim? Fortunately, we now know that we have first century records of integrity and historicity—the Gospels of Matthew, Mark, Luke and John. Through them we can step into the shoes of Jesus' disciples—the eyewitnesses—to discover the answer to this question. Their writings are clear—they all say that Jesus claimed to be both Messiah and God.

Making the DISCOVERY

The text of *FaithSearch* Discovery, *Surprised by Faith* (pp. 51-56) will help you to answer the questions and make the discovery in this chapter.

Introduction

In this chapter you will explore the evidence of Jesus' own claims to be Messiah and God. You will do that by taking a field trip back to the first century—using the ears of His disciples who were there.

Which one of these can be used as evidence in a court of law: an eyewitness account or hearsay (rumor, based not on personal knowledge but on another's statements)? [1] Why? (Review the quadrant on page 25 in chapter 3).

In your own words, express how what you have learned about the New Testament records in chapters 3 and 4 is now relevant to testing the claim that Jesus is God (review page 24 in SBF).

(2)True/False.   The first century eyewitness records of the New Testament meet the legal requirements for evidence that can be used to test the validity of Jesus' claims to be God.

How does this truth make it easier for you to defend Jesus' claim to be God than it would be for others who may have claimed deity in the past?

The disciples heard Jesus claim to be The Christ or Messiah

Read John 4:25-26 in a Bible, or in the margin of this page. In His conversation with the woman at the well in Samaria, who did Jesus tell her that He was?

The woman said to Him, "I know that Messiah is coming (He who is called Christ); when that One comes, He will declare all things to us." Jesus said to her, "I who speak to you am He."

—John 4:25-26

Locate Luke 24:25-27 and verse 46 in your Bible or in the margin of this page. Jesus had already suffered on the cross and had risen from the dead. In this passage, we read about a couple of His post-resurrection appearances to His disciples. As He talked to them, who does Jesus identify from Old Testament prophecy would need to suffer and rise again from the dead (verses 26 & 46)?

And He said to them, "O foolish men and slow of heart to believe in all that the prophets have spoken! Was it not necessary for the Christ to suffer these things and to enter into His glory?"

Then beginning with Moses and with all the prophets, He explained to them the things concerning Himself in all the Scriptures…. and He said to them, "Thus it is written, that the Christ would suffer and rise again from the dead the third day…"

—Luke 24:25-27,46

To whom did Jesus apply these prophecies? (verse 27)

Who, then, is Jesus claiming to be?

Read Mark 14:61-62 in a Bible, or in the margin of this page. When asked by the high priest Caiaphas if He was the Christ (Messiah), what did Jesus answer?

But He kept silent and did not answer. Again the high priest was questioning Him, and saying to Him, "Are You the Christ, the Son of the Blessed One?" And Jesus said, "I am; and you shall see the Son of Man sitting at the right hand of power, and coming with the clouds of heaven."

—Mark 14:61-62

It is clear from the biblical record that Jesus claimed to be the Messiah. What evidence links Jesus' life with the Messiah prophesied in the Old Testament? Read the summary below for help in formulating your answer. Look up some of the passages in your Bible to personally verify them.

One of the most persuasive lines of evidence that Jesus was the Messiah is that His life fulfilled numerous Old Testament prophecies. There are at least 456 Old Testament prophetic references that pertain to a future person that all were fulfilled in Jesus' life. Many of these He could not have any control over such as His place of birth. The following is a brief outline of some of these Old Testament prophecies and their New Testament fulfillment.

1. Jesus fulfilled the predicted family tree of the Messiah (Genesis 3:15; 49:10; Jeremiah 23:5-6; Matthew 1:20-23; 22:41-42)

2. Jesus fulfilled the predicted time of the coming of the Messiah (Daniel 9:25-26)

3. Jesus fulfilled the predicted details of the Messiah's life (selected examples from many):

    a. Bethlehem as birthplace (Micah 5:2 and Matthew 2:1-6)

    b. Born of a virgin (Isaiah 7:14 and Matthew 1:18-23)

c. Hands and feet would be pierced (Psalm 22:16 and John 20:25)

d. Betrayed for thirty pieces of silver (Zechariah 11:12ff and Matthew 26:14-16)

The odds that so many Old Testament prophecies would be fulfilled in one man are beyond imagination. What is the chance that any man might have lived from the day of these prophecies down to the present time and have fulfilled even eight of them? It has been estimated that the odds are one chance in 1017. Scientist Peter Stoner illustrated this probability:

> Suppose that we take 10^{17} silver dollars and lay them on the face of Texas. They will cover all of the state two feet deep. Now mark one of these silver dollars and stir the whole mass thoroughly, all over the state. Blindfold a man and tell him that he can travel as far as he wishes, but he must pick up one silver dollar and say that this is the right one. What chance would he have of getting the right one? Just the same chance that the prophets would have had of writing these eight prophecies and having them all come true in any one man, from their day to the present time, providing they wrote using their own wisdom (Peter W. Stoner, *Science Speaks* [Chicago: Moody Press, 1958], p.107).

The Christian religion began by the conversion of Jews from Judaism. A major argument that persuaded them was the evidence that Jesus' life was the fulfillment of Old Testament Messianic prophecy (Luke 24:25-27; John 5:46; Acts 8:30-35; 28:23). The apostles Peter, Paul, and John all taught that Jesus was the promised Messiah (Acts 2:36; 17:1-3; 1 John 2:22). There is overwhelming evidence to link Jesus' life with the prophesied Messiah.

(3)True/False. Jesus, the Christ (Messiah or "anointed one"), was prophesied in the Old Testament as both the One who would die for the sins of the people and who would reign forever as King on David's throne.

Read endnote number four on page 137 of SBF. Why is it reasonable to conclude that Jesus' claim to be the Messiah was also a claim to be Divine?

The disciples heard Jesus claim to be God on numerous occasions

Read the passages below in your Bible or in the margin of this page, regarding what Jesus' disciples recorded of His teachings. Write your answer to each question throughout this section.

Matthew 22:41-46

Jesus used a quote from the Psalmist, David, to confound the most educated and astute group in Israel, the Pharisees (SBF, p.53). He pointed out that in Psalm 110:1, David not only referred to the Messiah as being of Davidic descent, but also to be of (4) _____ origin. In other words, Jesus cited King David as saying here that his "son" (descendent) is also his (5) _____ !

Now while the Pharisees were gathered together, Jesus asked them a question: "What do you think about the Christ, whose son is He?" They said to Him, "The son of David." He said to them, "Then how does David in the Spirit call Him 'Lord,' saying, 'The Lord said to my Lord, "Sit at my right hand, until I put your enemies beneath your feet"'?

"If David then calls Him 'Lord,' how is He his son?"

No one was able to answer Him a word, nor did anyone dare from that day on to ask Him another question.

—Matthew 22:41-46

"Surely You are not greater than our father Abraham, who died? The prophets died too; whom do You make Yourself out to be?"

"Your father Abraham rejoiced to see My day, and he saw it and was glad."

So the Jews said to Him, "You are not yet fifty years old, and have You seen Abraham?"

Jesus said to them, "Truly, truly, I say to you, before Abraham was born, I AM."

Therefore they picked up stones to throw at Him, but Jesus hid Himself and went out of the temple.

        —John 8:53, 56-59

"I and the Father are one."

The Jews picked up stones again to stone Him.

Jesus answered them, "I showed you many good works from the Father; for which of them are you stoning Me?"

The Jews answered Him, "For a good work we do not stone You, but for blasphemy; and because You, being a man, make Yourself out to be God."

        —John 10:30-33

Jesus answered him, "It is written, 'You shall worship the Lord your God and serve Him only.'"

        —Luke 4:8

And he said, "Lord, I believe." And he worshiped Him.

        —John 9:38

And those who were in the boat worshiped Him, saying, "You are certainly God's Son!"

        —Matthew 14:33

When they saw Him, they worshiped Him; but some were doubtful.

        —Matthew 28:17

John 8:53, 56-59

Jesus claimed that His name is [6] ____ _____, the most intimate and personal name of God (SBF, p.53). The Jews tried to stone Him for what they thought was blasphemy. To speak blasphemy is to speak about God or sacred things with abuse or contempt, cursing or reviling God and being irreverent. (See Leviticus 24:16.)

John 10:30-33

Jesus claimed that He and the Father are [7] _____. Read the discussion of this verse on page 54 in SBF.

What are two possible meanings of "One" that *do not fit* either the grammar or the context of the verse?

What is the meaning of Jesus' claim to be "One" that *does fit* the grammar and context?

[8]True/False.   When Jesus claimed to be equal with the Father (John 10:30), the Jews tried to stone Him for what they believed was blasphemy.

Compare Luke 4:8 with John 9:38, Matthew 14:33 and 28:17 in your Bible or in the margin of this page. In what way do these passages indirectly support the contention that Jesus claimed to be God?

Jesus made the extraordinary claim that He was [9] _____ incarnate. The concept of the incarnation is the biblical teaching that God came to earth in the form of the man Jesus Christ who had both the nature of God and nature of man.

Is Jesus "God" or the "Son of God"? Sometimes people object that Jesus didn't actually claim to be God, but rather the Son of God. Read the discussion below for assistance in formulating an answer to this objection.

> Invariably when Jesus is discussed, someone will boldly proclaim that He wasn't actually God, but the Son of God. The contrast is unwarranted—it's not either/or but both/and. Jesus' identity as the Son of God includes having the same attributes as the Father, that is, He is from eternity, has all authority, etc. (see John 5:18). They are in essence, equal, as demonstrated in John 10:30 and claimed by Jesus in John 14:7-11. Jesus is also recorded as saying He has complete authority over heaven and earth (Matthew 28:18)

and that He alone is the means for people to know the Father (John 14:6).

Yet they are also separate persons of the Triune God. According to Matthew 11:27, Jesus taught that They enjoy a relationship that is unique and exclusive, i.e., no one else knows the Father as He does, and the Father knows Him as He knows no other. So intimate was His relationship that He never talked to His disciples about "our Father," but rather as "my Father" and "your Father" (John 20:17), and employed the family word "Abba" (daddy) when talking to Him.

However, it does not follow from such intimacy that Jesus is the "Son" of God in any literal, biological sense. Jesus was not conceived into existence for He existed eternally with the Father (John 1:1). His use of the term "Son" for Himself is to reflect a special relationship with the Father, not kinship.

Jesus is, nevertheless, the self-expression of God. As already cited above, He told Philip that "He who has seen me has seen the Father" (John 14:9). British theological scholar F.F. Bruce stated that, "The words He spoke, the works He performed, the life He led, the person He was—all disclosed the unseen Father. He is, in Paul's words, the visible 'image of the invisible God' (Colossians 1:15)" (F.F. Bruce, *Jesus: Lord and Savior* [InterVarsity Press, 1986], p.158).

Jesus shares the essence and nature of the one true God—He is not a secondary deity. "As the Son, He is the very expression of the Father; in Him we see the 'human face of God'" (Bruce, p.159).

A claim by Jesus to be God is consistent with the extreme reactions of those who heard Him

Jesus claimed He could give [(10)] _____ _____ to anyone (John 5:21). Only God has this authority and power.

Jesus claimed that He was [(11)] "from _____" and "not of this _____" (John 8:23-24). He also said that anyone who does not believe that He is God will die in their sins.

If Jesus truly made the two claims above, then it is abundantly clear they are stupendous in nature. Imagine yourself making similar claims to your family and friends. Describe how you think they would respond: smile and encourage you, or become concerned and even suggest counseling?

The degree of reaction of the hearer can often be an indicator of the nature of the claim being made. Read the passages below in your Bible or in the margin of this page, and write down the reactions of those who heard what Jesus said.

John 5:17-18

John 8:58-59

Mark 14:60-64

Would you consider these reactions to be extreme?

"For just as the Father raises the dead and gives them life, even so the Son also gives life to whom He wishes." **—John 5:21**

And He was saying to them, "You are from below, I am from above; you are of this world, I am not of this world. Therefore I said to you that you will die in your sins; for unless you believe that I am He, you will die in your sins." **—John 8:23-24**

The high priest stood up and came forward and questioned Jesus, saying, "Do You not answer? What is it that these men are testifying against You?"

But He kept silent and did not answer. Again the high priest was questioning Him, and saying to Him, "Are You the Christ, the Son of the Blessed One?"

And Jesus said, "I am; and you shall see the Son of Man sitting at the right hand of power, and coming with the clouds of heaven."

Tearing his clothes, the high priest said, "What further need do we have of witnesses? You have heard the blasphemy; how does it seem to you?" And they all condemned Him to be deserving of death.

—Mark 14:60-64

Do you think these reactions are indicative of and consistent with the contention that Jesus was claiming to be God?

Do you agree that Jesus' statements are not what you expect a person who is merely a human being to say?

What would it take for you to convince your family and friends that you were God?

What insight does this give you into Jesus' own situation?

(12)True/False. The extreme reactions of those who were eyewitnesses of Jesus (like putting Him to death) reinforce the fact that His claims about Himself were extraordinary.

Read the discussion below for background to those who were Jesus' primary opponents: the Pharisees, Sadducees and scribes.

> A significant change from the close of the Old Testament to Jesus' time was the presence of several new Jewish sects and political parties.
>
> The Pharisees were the largest group, numbering approximately six thousand. They were strict nationalists originating as the Hasidim ("the Pious") who joined the Maccabean revolt in the third century before Christ to resist the Hellenization of (Greek influence on) Jewish culture. They are best known in the New Testament by their excessive legalistic observance of the rabbinic and Mosaic laws, and were often criticized by Jesus for being blind to the spirit of the law (Matthew 23). Their activities centered in the synagogue; they believed in the immortality of the soul and a bodily resurrection, salvation by good works, and the existence of a hierarchy of angels and demons.
>
> The Sadducees originated simultaneously with the Pharisees as those supportive of Greek thought and culture. They claimed Zadok the Davidic high priest as their ancestor, so their activities were centered in the Temple. While the Pharisees were middle-class laymen, the Sadducees were priestly aristocrats of wealth and affluence, wielding considerable political influence. They were not as popular with the common people as the Pharisees. They taught that there is no personal immortality nor resurrection, denied the existence of angels and demons, and insisted on the absolute free will of humans to determine the course of history.
>
> The scribes (lawyers, teachers and doctors of the law) were a professional group rather than a religious sect or political party. Thus, they could belong to any group, though by Jesus' time probably most scribes were Pharisees. Their role was to be experts in the Old Testament law which was the law of the

land. This included teaching, interpreting the law for application to daily life, and delivering judicial pronouncements on difficult cases. They were primarily responsible for the Pharisaic oral traditions referred to as the "traditions of the elders" (Mark 7:3-13). Sometimes people referred to Jesus using the title of "Rabbi" (Matthew 26:25; Mark 9:5), which is a form of Pharisaic or scribal identity; but He was clearly distinct from both of these groups in His teaching style (Matthew 7:28-29).

A claim by Jesus to be God explains some difficult Old Testament statements

There are certain Old Testament passages that state the Messiah would be divine or God. He would be "from the days of eternity" (Micah 5:2) and would bear the name of God ("Lord"=Adonai, Matthew 22:44). He would be called "Mighty God" and "Eternal Father" (Isaiah 9:6-7). If Jesus as the Messiah is also God, then certain difficult biblical statements are clarified.

For example, in Zechariah 12:10 God declares

"…they will look on Me whom they have pierced…"

When was God ever pierced?

If Jesus is God, how would that help explain this passage?

In Revelation 1:8, 17-18 we read: "'I am the Alpha and the Omega,' says the Lord God, 'who is and who was and who is to come, the Almighty. …I am the first and the last, and the living One; and I was dead, and behold, I am alive forevermore…'"

When did God die?

If Jesus is God, how would that help explain this passage?

In Psalm 16:10 God says, "For You will not abandon my soul to Sheol; Nor will You allow Your Holy One to undergo decay."

When was God put in the grave?

If Jesus is God, how would that help explain this passage?

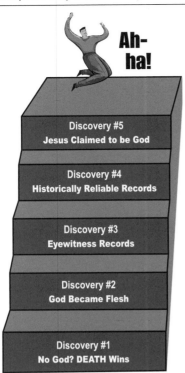

Ah-ha!

Discovery #5
Jesus Claimed to be God

Discovery #4
Historically Reliable Records

Discovery #3
Eyewitness Records

Discovery #2
God Became Flesh

Discovery #1
No God? DEATH Wins

No man can by any means redeem his brother, Or give to God a ransom for him (Psalm 49:7). "For even the Son of Man did not come to be served, but to serve, and to give His life a ransom for many" (Mark 10:45).
—Psalm 49:7 with Mark 10:45

"My sheep hear My voice, and I know them, and they follow Me; and I give eternal life to them, and they will never perish; and no one will snatch them out of My hand."
—John 10:27-28

And he said, "Lord, I believe." And he worshipped Him.
—John 9:38

But the eleven disciples proceeded to Galilee, to the mountain which Jesus had designated. When they saw Him, they worshiped Him; but some were doubtful.
—Matthew 28:16-17

"But as for you, Bethlehem…From you One will go forth for Me to be ruler in Israel. His goings forth are from long ago, From the days of eternity" (Micah 5:2). *For a child will be born to us, a son will be given to us…And His name will be called Wonderful Counselor, Mighty God, Eternal Father, Prince of Peace* (Isaiah 9:6).
—Micah 5:2 and Isaiah 9:6

All the lines of evidence and biblical passages explored in this chapter have revealed our fifth *FaithSearch* Discovery.

Ah-ha!
The DISCOVERY
Eyewitnesses testified that Jesus claimed to be God!

Application and Reflection

Do you agree that the question of whether Jesus actually was God is the most significant issue of Christianity's validity? Why or why not?

Were Jesus' exclusive claims to be God as presented in this chapter convincing to you?

If not, why not? What evidence would be convincing to you?

Confirming the Discovery

Read the references below in a Bible, or as provided here in the margin. Write below how the main teaching of each relates to or confirms the discovery made in this chapter.

Psalm 49:7 with Mark 10:45

John 10:27-28

John 9:38 and Matthew 28:16-17

Micah 5:2 with Isaiah 9:6

In summary of God's Word, the Old and New Testaments are clear that the promised Messiah would be both man and God. Jesus claimed that He gave His life as a ransom for sin, but God says in Psalm 49:7 that no man can redeem the life of another or ransom them. Hence, Jesus must be claiming to be more than a man and without sin as no other man ever was or is. By claiming that He could give and guarantee eternal life to His followers (John 10:27-28), Jesus was promising what only a God with absolute power and authority could deliver. During His temptations in the wilderness Jesus stated that only God must be worshiped (Luke 4:8). His acceptance of worship without objection during His ministry is an indirect way of claiming divinity (John 9:38; Matthew 28:16-17). A child would be born in Galilee of the Gentiles who would be called "Mighty God" and "Eternal Father" (Isaiah 9:6). Little Bethlehem would deliver a ruler of Israel who is "from the days of eternity" (Micah 5:2). Jesus fulfills them both—Son of Man and Lord God!

Looking Ahead

Why should we believe Jesus when He claims to be God? Surely some other people have claimed the same thing. What makes Jesus different? We will find out in the next chapter.

Answers for the objective questions in this chapter:

1. eyewitness account	2. True	3. True	4. divine
5. God	6. I AM	7. One	8. True
9. God	10. eternal life	11. above; world	12. True

CHAPTER 6

Revealing the Truth About Jesus

Discovering that Jesus' Miracles and Resurrection Substantiate His Claim to be God

Getting FOCUSED

- How could Jesus be sane while claiming to be God?
- Were Jesus' miracles real or just magic?
- Was the resurrection of Jesus fact or fiction?

A Leader's Guide is available with answers to these questions, guidelines for leading small group interaction, and other helpful resources. It's available free by downloading it from the **FaithSearch** Web site (www.faithsearch.org). For a small fee plus postage, a printed copy can be requested from the **FaithSearch** office (952-401-4501).

Chapter 5 discussed the evidence that Jesus truly did claim to be God, and that those who heard Him—both friends and enemies—understood that to be His meaning. Given these claims, what is the most reasonable option concerning Jesus' true identity? Is He only a legend? No. We have discovered that the New Testament Gospels are first century eyewitness accounts, *not* legendary fabrications written down after generations of oral tradition embellished in the telling. Is He a liar or a lunatic? Or, is He the Lord He claimed to be? On what basis can we decide among these options? Those who were with Him accurately recorded the historical evidence from His life which enables us to answer these questions with certainty.

Making the DISCOVERY

The text of *FaithSearch* Discovery, *Surprised by Faith* (pp. 57-69) will help you to answer the questions and make the discovery in this chapter.

Introduction

The evidence of Jesus' actions that backed up His claim to be God is recorded in the biblical Gospels. Read the following passages in your Bible and record how people responded when they met and observed Jesus during His ministry 2,000 years ago.

John 4:7-29

John 4:46-53

John 6:1-14

John 9:1-38

John 11:14-27

John 20:24-29

Therefore many other signs Jesus also performed in the presence of the disciples, which are not written in this book; but these have been written so that you may believe that Jesus is the Christ, the Son of God; and that believing you may have life in His name.

—John 20:30-31

And there are also many other things which Jesus did, which if they were written in detail, I suppose that even the world itself would not contain the books that would be written.

—John 21:25

Read John 20:30-31 and 21:25 in a Bible, or in the margin of this page. Did John include every miracle of Jesus in his record? Why did he include the ones that he did? Do they help you to believe that Jesus is who He claimed to be?

Historical Evidence that Jesus is God

Jesus is named "Lord" in the New Testament, for example, by Thomas (John 20:27-28). This is translated from the Greek word "Kurios" which means "supreme one" and is equivalent to God. What did Jesus do that convinced people He was indeed Lord? (See the chart, SBF, p. 63.)

For your answer, complete the statements below by filling in the blanks.

Jesus demonstrated His authority to [1] _____ _____ and heal sickness (Luke 5:17-26). Removal of the man's paralysis proved to the Jews that Jesus removed the sin that, in their minds, caused it. Consistent with the Jews' own declaration, only God can forgive offenses done against Him.

Jesus demonstrated His authority over [2] _____ (Luke 7:11-16). When humankind confronts death, death always wins. Jesus confronted death—and won! Only God could have power over death and give eternal life in its place.

Jesus also demonstrated His authority over [3] _____ (Luke 8:22-25). Scientists refer to the "laws" of nature, but Jesus had control over them because as God, He was the "law-maker."

Jesus further demonstrated His authority over [4] _____ _____ (Luke 4:33-36). The people asked, "What is this message?" This means, "What does this miracle tell us about who He is?" Only God or the head of the demons would have the authority and power to do this. Jesus told them how foolish it was to think His power was other than that of God (Matthew 12:24-29).

[5] True/False. In backing up His claims to be God, Jesus failed to show His control over natural law.

"If I do not do the works of My Father, do not believe Me; but if I do them, though you do not believe Me, believe the works, so that you may know and understand that the Father is in Me, and I in the Father."

—John 10:37-38

As you have just identified above, eyewitnesses to Jesus reported that He had authority over demons, death, sickness and nature, and that He could forgive and remove the consequences of sin. Explain briefly why these historical acts of Jesus are important for determining His identity as God. (See John 10:37-38 in a Bible or in the margin of this page and SBF, pp.68-69.)

Suppose you were told of a spectacular account of someone who was healed of terminal cancer, but you had not witnessed it yourself. On what basis or for what reasons might you accept that it really happened? Read the discussion below for additional perspective in formulating your answer.

Some people wonder, "If miracles are real, why don't we see them today?" To many people, the world they live in seems to have no divine intervention, no interruptions to the natural order, and the dead stay dead. As far as they are concerned the many miracles of the Bible seem more like fairy tales than truth.

What is a miracle? One source defines a miracle as a "divine intervention into, or interruption of, the regular course of the world that produces a purposeful but unusual event that would not have occurred otherwise" (Norman Geisler and Ron Brooks, *When Skeptics Ask*, [Wheaton: Victor Books, 1990], p. 76). This does not mean that miracles are a violation of natural law. Rather, they have a cause that transcends nature.

Are miracles possible? Yes, if God exists. Obviously, you cannot believe miracles have happened without believing that a being powerful enough to do miracles exists. Besides, natural laws do not tell us what must happen all the time, only what happens under certain circumstances or at certain times. If there is an all-powerful God outside the universe who can change circumstances and conditions in the universe, then miracles are possible. Furthermore, the timing and frequency of miracles is then God's choice. He has chosen to intervene in nature at certain times for a purpose. One of those times was in the life of Jesus to authenticate Him as God. Because God doesn't choose to do a miracle in my experience, then, doesn't mean miracles aren't possible.

But are miracles credible? Since most people don't experience a miracle, some people conclude that anyone who claims to have experienced a miracle is not credible. The error in logic here is that this view equates evidence with probability, that is, you can't believe Jesus' claim to have raised the dead because most people aren't raised.

Under this view, you could never believe someone's claim to have won the lottery because most people don't win. In contrast, belief in miracles should be based on an open investigation of the eyewitness accounts of historical facts, not probabilities. They are events—and events can be investigated using legal evidence to determine their credibility, whether affirmative or negative.

To speak quite frankly, sometimes Christians are rather careless in their reference to "miracles" happening in their life and circumstances. Often, a miracle as defined above is not what is meant nor has one occurred. However, at times there are reported events even today that when investigated factually, prove to fit the definition of a miracle. Furthermore, every person who has repented of their sin and confessed their faith in Jesus Christ has a miracle of new life created within them (John 1:12-13; 2 Corinthians 5:17). This experience affirms for them that miracles are not only possible, but actually happen today.

For more information on miracles, see Geisler and Brooks, *When Skeptics Ask*, pp. 75-99; Lee Strobel, *The Case for Faith* (Grand Rapids: Zondervan Publishing, 2000), pp. 57-86; and
C.S. Lewis, *Miracles: A Preliminary Study* (New York: Macmillan, 1947).

There are people in the world today who question the truth concerning Jesus. Some of their objections are listed below. After reading the discussion associated with each objection, write your own brief response as if you were answering someone who expressed that objection to you.

Three Objections to the Historical Evidence

Objection #1

According to the Old Testament, some of the prophets performed miracles, too (e.g., Elijah in 1 Kings 17-18). Why don't we think this demonstrates that Elijah is God? How is this any different from Jesus? Read the discussion below for assistance in answering this objection.

Do the prophets' miracles indicate their deity? Clarence Benson in his *Biblical Beliefs* (Wheaton: ETTA, 1962, vol. 2, p. 11) says that the phrase, "Thus saith the Lord" occurs about 1,900 times in the Old Testament. Other expressions such as, "the Lord said," "the Lord spoke," and "the Word of the Lord came," are found 3,808 times. The Old Testament prophets were extremely careful and insistent that they spoke only what God told them, and that they were only the instruments through which God manifested His power to do miracles.

No Old Testament prophet ever claimed to be God. In contrast, Jesus did claim to be God, and often spoke as God: "I am the way, and the truth, and the life" (John 14:6); "I am the resurrection and the life" (John 11:25); "I am the bread of life" (John 6:35); and "I am the door of the sheep" (John 10:7). Jesus' claims and actions are in the first person as if God Himself were speaking. They do not allow Him to be identified as only a prophet through whom God worked.

That is the authority which the Jews recognized in Jesus as recorded in Matthew 7:28-29: "...the crowds were amazed at His teaching; for He was teaching them as one have authority, and not as their scribes." If Jesus were only a prophet, then His divine claims and actions could be seen as justification for the Jewish leadership to call Him a blasphemer and demand His death according to the Law.

On the other hand, they should have recognized that Jesus' miraculous actions vindicated His claims to be God. That is, He walked the talk! (See SBF, pp. 61-63.)

Objection #2

How do we know that Jesus wasn't just a magician, fooling people into thinking He did miracles? Read the discussion below for assistance in answering this objection.

Even with all of our advanced theatrical technology today we cannot begin to come close to duplicating the miracles of Jesus through the art of illusion or some type of magic trick. The miracles of Jesus were performed nearly 2,000 years ago in the midst of an open desert. To accomplish these effects through

theatrical tricks would require literally tons of equipment (e.g. lighting, special staging, elaborate props, etc.). Jesus demonstrated powers over the elements, matter, time, space and even over life and death. Only the *creator* of life and the universe could demonstrate such *power over* life and the universe.

Many professional magicians and illusionists have investigated the miraculous activity of Jesus of Nazareth and have arrived at the same conclusion. Andre Kole (the world-famous creator of stage illusions for such artists as David Copperfield and Siegfried & Roy) states, "If Jesus Christ was a magician, then His illusions were totally different from anything any other magicians have done before or since" (Andre Kole, *Miracles or Magic* [Eugene, OR: Harvest House, 1987], p. 109).

If the devil and spirit mediums all claim to do supernatural feats, why would the fact that Jesus did miracles prove that He was God? Read the discussion below for assistance in answering this objection.

Objection 3

Can the supernatural be distinguished from the miraculous? If the devil and mediums all claim to do supernatural feats, why would the fact that Jesus did miracles prove that He is God? Certainly the devil (a fallen angel, according to the biblical record) and mediums are involved in supernatural activity, but that does not equate to being miraculous. The terms "supernatural" and "miraculous" are not completely interchangeable. The Bible refers to the genuine miraculous only as it is linked to God as the Author of the miracles. Dr. Norm Geisler articulates this well: "In spite of Satan's super power, he cannot do truly supernatural things as God can do. For example, he cannot create life or raise the dead" (Norman Geisler, *Signs and Wonders* [Wheaton, IL: Tyndale House, 1988], p. 104).

According to the Bible, Satan and his legions certainly do have powers. However, those powers have limits and are fueled through lies and deception (John 8:44). The realm of the genuine miraculous belongs to God alone. Consider the following passages. In Exodus 15:11, Moses and the sons of Israel are found singing to the Lord in rhetorical questions: "Who is like You among the gods, O Lord? Who is like You, majestic in holiness, Awesome in praises, working wonders [or working miracles]?" The obvious answer to that question is: No one!

In Psalm 72:18, Solomon declares, "Blessed be the Lord God, the God of Israel, Who alone works wonders." Then again in Psalm 136:3-4, the psalmist declares, "Give thanks to the Lord of lords, For His lovingkindness is everlasting. To Him who alone does great wonders..." Notice that the attribute of God being praised here is that *God alone works wonders*. The original Hebrew word for "alone" can also be expressed in the word "solitary."

Dr. Louis Goldberg, Professor of Theology and Jewish Studies at Moody Bible Institute, has written that the word "alone," as found in the passage above, "is used of the Lord's incomparability and uniqueness in His exclusive claim to deity as seen in his extra-ordinary works" (*Theological*

Wordbook of the Old Testament, [Chicago: Moody Press, 1980]).

Therefore, if God is the only source for the genuinely miraculous, and Jesus presented genuine miracles—then He must certainly be equal in essence to God.

Historical Evidence for Jesus' Resurrection

Without question, the historical resurrection of Jesus was the capstone evidence of His deity, both for Jesus' contemporaries and for us today. What is the evidence that has made the truth of Jesus' resurrection from the grave so compelling? (See SBF, pp.65-68.)

The [6] _____ tomb. Jesus' body was no longer in the tomb on the third day after His death.

The [7] _____ to eyewitnesses. Friends and foes testified they saw Jesus alive physically on several occasions subsequent to His death.

The [8] _____ lives of the disciples. They were fearful and in hiding after Jesus' death, but following His resurrection, they became bold witnesses—even willing to become martyrs for the truth.

[9] In summary, the evidence for the fact and truth of Jesus' resurrection include:

    a) the empty tomb
    b) the appearances to eyewitnesses
    c) the transformed lives of the disciples
    d) all of the above.

Objections to Jesus' Resurrection

There are some people who question whether Jesus really rose physically from the dead. Why do you suppose this is? Do they base their view on the evidence? Read the discussion below for insight to formulating your answer.

There have been many theories attempting to explain away the facts of Jesus' empty tomb: a) The Swoon theory—Jesus didn't actually die on the cross and He resuscitated in the cool tomb. His disciples then deceptively proclaimed His resurrection; b) The Conspiracy theory—the disciples stole the body and deceptively proclaimed his resurrection; c) The Jewish authorities removed the body unknown to the disciples, who mistakenly thought He had resurrected; d) The Wrong Tomb theory—the women and the disciples went to the wrong tomb and mistakenly thought He was resurrected; e) The Legend Theory—the disciples left Jerusalem for a long time and much later returned to propagate an imaginary myth of resurrection; f) The Hallucination Theory—the disciples had hallucinations in which they imagined seeing the resurrected Jesus. They then proclaimed His resurrection.

There are several problems that destroy most of these arguments. For example, these theories accept *some* aspects of the historical record and arbitrarily and inconsistently reject *other* parts. All but the legend and hallucination theories have been abandoned by most contemporary historians and theologians.

Some, like Muslims, deny that it was Jesus Himself who was crucified. They maintain that it was someone who looked like Him or it was Simon the Cyrenian (Luke 23:26) or otherwise. Others maintain that Jesus had a twin who pretended to be the resurrected Jesus after the crucifixion. Still others simply reject the resurrection by maintaining that Jesus' body was dumped outside the city walls and eaten by wild dogs.

All these views fail when we remember that the Gospel records are eyewitness accounts and their teaching about Jesus was accepted by many Jews in Jerusalem who were in the best position to know whether or not they were telling the truth—and had a great deal to lose if they chose to believe it and follow Jesus. The fact that they did so in spite of the risk is powerful testimony that it must have been undeniably true. Consider the disciples. Why would they be willing to die for their faith (most became martyrs) if they knew the resurrection to be a hoax? If Jesus' enemies stole His body, all they would have had to do to discredit Him and His followers would be to produce it.

(10) The most compelling evidence that Jesus truly is God:

    a) His compassion
    b) His claims
    c) His sincerity
    d) His resurrection

(11) True/False.   Jesus accurately predicted His own death and resurrection (Matthew 16:21).

Options for Jesus' Identity

The evidence of Jesus' claims, miracles and resurrection is the basis for a conclusion about His identity. A verdict is a conclusion based on legal evidence, beyond a reasonable doubt. What options do we have as we consider a verdict about who Jesus is? In the blanks below, fill in the three possible options. (See SBF, pp.64-65.)

1. Jesus is a (12) _LIAR_ . Jesus cannot be thought of as a great moral teacher and simultaneously be identified as the greatest liar who ever lived (based on the billions of people who would have allegedly been deceived). This option is false because His character throughout the historical accounts supports a person of the highest virtue and integrity. This option is also false because it is inconceivable that Jesus could sustain a committed following for several years without being detected as a fraud. Thirdly, this option is false because He was authenticated as genuine by His resurrection from the dead.

2. Jesus is a (13) _LUNATIC_ . If Jesus really thought He was God, but wasn't, He'd have to be severely mentally deluded. This option is false because Jesus manifested no symptoms of psychiatric disorders. Rather, He demonstrated qualities of excellent mental health. This option is also

false because He was authenticated as genuine by His resurrection from the dead.

3. Jesus is [14] _LORD_ . This option is most consistent with His claims and the evidence of His actions already considered. It is also true because there can be no greater credential to authenticate Jesus' claim to be God than the objective eyewitness evidence of His physical resurrection.

In summary, of the points just discussed, which options can logically be included concerning the question, "Who is Jesus?":[15]

a) lunatic
b) great moral teacher, but not God
c) liar
d) Lord
e) all of the above.

The fact that the New Testament records were written within the lifetime of the eyewitnesses of Jesus eliminates the view that Jesus is: [16] (see SBF, p.64)

a) the Lord
b) a liar
c) a legend
d) a lunatic
e) none of the above.

Therefore, the conclusion most consistent with the evidence considered in this chapter is our sixth *FaithSearch* discovery.

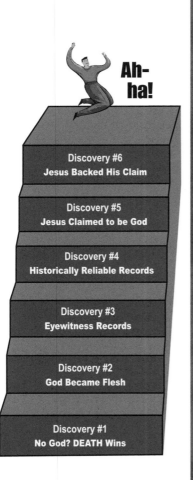

Ah-ha!

Discovery #6
Jesus Backed His Claim

Discovery #5
Jesus Claimed to be God

Discovery #4
Historically Reliable Records

Discovery #3
Eyewitness Records

Discovery #2
God Became Flesh

Discovery #1
No God? DEATH Wins

Ah-ha!
The DISCOVERY

The compelling evidence of Jesus' miracles and resurrection from the dead confirmed His claim to be God!

Application and Reflection

Sometimes people ask, "Why are there four different Gospels about Jesus in the New Testament? Isn't that confusing?" How would you answer? Read the discussion below for assistance and then write two or more points in formulating your answer.

There is a sense in which the question ought to be, "Why are there *only* four Gospels?" The life, ministry, death and resurrection of Jesus Christ have had the greatest impact on humanity of any event in history! How can these short accounts do justice to something so important? As John the apostle said at the close of his Gospel, "And there are also many other things which Jesus did, which if they were written in detail, I suppose that even the world itself would not contain the books that would be written" (John 21:25). Therefore, even four accounts are not enough, but these do give us a four-dimensional portrait of Jesus. The Gospels of Matthew, Mark, Luke and John were written by eyewitness apostles or their associates. They were evangelists and desired to present whatever part of Jesus' ministry and teaching that would appeal to the particular audience they were trying to reach. They are not repetitious chronological biographies of Jesus' life. Each Gospel has a distinct purpose, identifiable audience and individual characteristics which are evident in their contents. Each contributes a significant, supplemental, true dimension to our understanding of Jesus. The first three Gospels, Matthew, Mark and Luke, are called the synoptics—coming from a Greek word meaning "viewed together." They present the life of Christ in similar ways with a lot of parallel content.

In Matthew, Jesus is the royal Jewish Messiah and eternal King, in fulfillment of Old Testament prophecy. It was probably written to present Jesus to the Jews and teach them in the faith after their commitment to follow Him. Mark's Gospel presents Jesus as the divine Servant-Worker and Redeemer. The action-packed ministry of Jesus which was characterized by His powerful but humble service would be appealing to the Gentiles, particularly Romans. Finally, the portrait of Jesus in the third synoptic Gospel is that of the universal, ideal and perfect man—the cosmopolitan and sympathetic Savior of all mankind. Jesus' inclusion in His Kingdom of the Gentiles, social outcasts, women and children would be particularly appealing to the Greeks of that day.

The Gospel of John distinctly states that it was written to lead the reader to saving faith in Jesus the Messiah, God's Son (20:30-31). Over 90 percent of its content is not found in the three synoptic Gospels. John's narrative includes seven miracles, over twenty testimonies of people who met Jesus, numerous titles and claims of Jesus—all supporting the significant truth of the deity of Jesus as the unique and preexistent Son of God.

The uniqueness of each Gospel was symbolized early in Church history when the four were identified with the images of a lion, ox, human being and eagle, respectively. Therefore, we are not limited to one perspective on Jesus, but have the richness of four.

Suppose you had been with Jesus in the region of Caesarea Philippi (Matthew 16:13-15), heard Him teach and saw the miracles He did. Then He turned to you and asked, "But who do you say that I am?" What do you think you would have said then? How would you answer Him now?

Confirming the Discovery

Read the references below in a Bible, or as provided here in the margin. Write after each one how it relates to or confirms the discovery made in this chapter.

John 10:37-38

"If I do not do the works of My Father, do not believe Me; but if I do them, though you do not believe Me, believe the works, that you may know and understand that the Father is in Me, and I in the Father."

—John 10:37-38

Therefore many other signs [miracles] Jesus also performed in the presence of the disciples, which are not written in this book; but these have been written so that you may believe that Jesus is the Christ, the Son of God; and that believing you may have life in His name.
—John 20:30-31

God… in these last days has spoken to us in His Son, whom He appointed heir of all things, through whom also He made the world. And He is the radiance of His glory and the exact representation of His nature, and upholds all things by the word of His power. When He had made purification of sins, He sat down at the right hand of the Majesty on high…
—Hebrews 1:1-3

"I am the Alpha and the Omega," says the Lord God, "who is and who was and who is to come, the Almighty. …I am the first and the last, and the living One; and I was dead, and behold, I am alive forevermore…"
—Revelation 1:8, 17-18

John 20:30-31

Hebrews 1:1-3

Revelation 1:8, 17-18

In summary of God's Word, Jesus taught that "every good tree bears good fruit" (Matthew 7:17). Likewise, He taught that we should recognize Him as the true Son of God because He did the works (miracles and teaching of truth) of His Father (John 10:37-38). The apostle John acknowledged that Jesus did many more miracles than are recorded in our Gospels. He also stated that the miracles should lead us to faith and eternal life in Him (John 20:30-31). In an incredible summary of Jesus' identity, the writer of Hebrews described Him as the Son of God, God's heir, creator of the world, truly God just like His Father, sustainer of the creation, redeemer of humanity, and ultimate judge with His Father (Hebrews 1:1-3). God spoke through the apostle John and said that He was dead and is alive again (Revelation 1:8, 17-18)! When did God die? This can only be explained if He is referring to Jesus' death and resurrection. This proves that Jesus is God.

Looking Ahead

The implication of the truth we have considered in this chapter is that each of us is faced with the decision to (17) _____ or (18) _____ Jesus as Lord of our life. (See diagram, SBF, p.65.)

(19) True/False.   As personal beings, we were created with free will. This means that each of us will be held accountable for the individual choice we make concerning Jesus; that is, we either accept Him by a personal confession of faith or we reject Him as our Savior and Lord.

Of course, this choice leads us to the question of "faith." How do you get faith? Can faith be reasonable? Is faith just wishful thinking or can it be a certainty? What makes faith valid? These are the important questions we will explore in the next chapter.

Answers for the objective questions in this chapter:

1. forgive sins	2. death	3. nature
4. demonic spirits	5. False	6. empty
7. appearances	8. transformed	9. d
10. d	11. True	12. liar
13. lunatic	14. Lord	15. a, c, d
16. c	17. accept	18. reject
19. True		

CHAPTER 7

What Makes Faith Valid?

Discovering the Teaching of the Bible on this Often-Misunderstood Subject

Getting FOCUSED

- Is faith blind, a mere holding on to what you know isn't true?
- Does it matter what you believe as long as you are sincere in that belief?
- How is Christian faith different from that of other religions?

Faith is often caricatured in society as anti-intellectual and a crutch for the weak. Sometimes this caricature is established in the minds of people by the media's coverage of a few fanatical people who misrepresent faith, or by personal experience with those who fail to live out their faith consistently. In contrast, the Bible teaches that Christian faith is intellectually reasonable and logically valid because it is based on a proven and trustworthy object—the person of Jesus Christ. No one needs to "check their brain at the door" of the Christian faith.

Making the DISCOVERY

The text of *FaithSearch* Discovery, *Surprised by Faith* (pp. 71-83 and 91-103) will help you to answer the questions and make the discovery in this chapter.

Introduction

Some time ago a Christian couple whom I knew received a handwritten letter from their unbelieving friends. They were very direct in their written expression: "We have had it up to our ears with dogmatic mystical people whose beliefs are not based on any real reasons and evidence…. We think you are all brainwashed, gullible and narrow-minded. You cannot verify in any way your hysterical beliefs."

It's my hope that it is obvious to you at this point in *FaithSearch* Discovery, that this couple's view represents some level of ignorance and a serious misunderstanding of the Christian faith (SBF, p. 71). We identified several stereotypes and caricatures of religion and faith in chapter 1. But this unbelieving couple made reference to yet another serious allegation against Christianity: narrow-minded and exclusive beliefs.

Is there truth to their allegation? Is Christianity more exclusive than other religions by claiming that Jesus is the only way to God? Prepare a short answer to this allegation after you have read the selection below for assistance.

A Leader's Guide is available with answers to these questions, guidelines for leading small group interaction, and other helpful resources. It's available free by downloading it from the *FaithSearch* Web site (www.faithsearch.org). For a small fee plus postage, a printed copy can be requested from the *FaithSearch* office (952-401-4501).

This question raises two related issues. First, is it true that the Christian faith maintains that the only way of salvation is through faith in Jesus Christ? Yes, but it is not arbitrary: there are important reasons. The first reason is that the founder of Christianity, Jesus Christ, taught this Himself. He said, "I am the way, and the truth, and the life; no one comes to the Father, but through Me" (John 14:6). On another occasion He taught that "no one knows the Father except the Son and those to whom the Son chooses to reveal Him" (Matthew 11:27, NIV). Furthermore, those who received their instruction in the faith from Jesus Himself also taught this. The apostles Peter and John said, "Salvation is found in no one else, for there is no other name under heaven given to men by which we must be saved" (Acts 4:12, NIV).

Finally, there is a vital theological reason why Jesus is the only way. Someone has to remove the sin in our lives that separates us from a holy God. Only Jesus, the sinless incarnate God-man, was qualified to do this by his substitutionary death on the cross. Jesus is the only way because He alone provided the "only way." A more detailed explanation of this will be given in chapter 8.

The second issue of this question is whether Christianity is more exclusive in its claims than other religions. Actually not, since all the major religions make exclusive claims. According to Muslims, Jesus was a failure and Muhammad was a success; the Qu'ran stands alone (in Arabic) as the culminating point of divine revelation; and those outside their faith are infidels. According to orthodox Judaism, Jews are the exclusive people of God; God is one and not a Trinity; they need no redemption from sin outside the provisions of the Law; and Jesus is not the promised Messiah. Hinduism is insistent on an impersonal Brahman as god and the law of karma and reincarnation as the way to "salvation."

All religions have exclusive claims but may seem more tolerant than Christianity because they share a common view that good deeds are the basis for individuals to achieve approval with their god. Other religions may differ from each other as to which deeds provide the greatest merit, but most agree that people can earn salvation by their individual effort and virtue. This is self-assuring to proud people and gives a sense of acceptance and accomplishment, placing people's efforts as the central focus. Since Christianity doesn't recognize human merit to earn heaven, but teaches that entrance is by confession of sin and faith in the person and work of Jesus only, it is perceived as personally depreciating, restrictive and narrow-minded. In essence, the Christian faith is really more inclusive than others because it offers forgiveness and adoption into the family of God to everyone without regard to wealth, social rank, race, accomplishments, etc. Christianity is unique and offers the assurance of life after death on the basis of mercy and grace alone.

"For God so loved the world, that He gave His only begotten Son, that whoever believes [has faith] in Him shall not perish, but have eternal life" (emphasis added).
—**John 3:16**

The word "faith" in the New Testament is the translation of the Greek "pistis," a (1) __NOUN__ form, and "believe" is the translation of the Greek "pisteuo," a (2) __VERB__ form (SBF, p. 73). They only differ grammatically, not theologically, in their meaning. Read John 3:16 in the margin of this page. From the explanation of the noun and verb forms of faith just given, read it once using "believes" and again using "has faith." Why does this substitution not change the essential meaning of "trust" in this or other Bible passages?

The Essential Components of Faith

We have all said or heard someone else say, "I believe." An obvious response to this statement might be: "Believe in what?" If the person says, "In nothing," then for them "I believe" is only a statement about how they feel, about the state of their will, or that they are trusting in "faith" itself. What *should* they say in answer to this question? What are the essential components to having a faith as depicted in the Bible?

The Bible identifies [3] ___KNOWLEDGE___ as an essential component of faith (SBF, p. 73).

[4] Place a check mark before the correct statement:

____ Faith is in NOTHING

_✓_ Faith is in SOMETHING

This is the meaning of "knowledge" in the first essential component of faith. It is whatever you place after "I believe in"_____ –the "something" in which you are trusting. It might be the chair you sit on, the car you drive, the bungee cord that is strapped to your body, or a person.

Read Romans 10:13-15 in a Bible or the margin of this page. Identify the logical sequence in this passage by answering the questions below.

Who will be saved?

Who will call?

Who will believe?

How will they hear?

What must be done with those who tell (preach)?

If you had an opportunity to ask the apostle Paul, based on his teaching here, "Is it necessary to hear in order to believe (have faith)?" what do you think he would say? (See Romans 10:17.)

Essential Component of Faith #1

...for "Whoever will call on the name of the Lord will be saved." How then will they call on Him in whom they have not believed? How will they believe in Him whom they have not heard? And how will they hear without a preacher? How will they preach unless they are sent? Just as it is written, "How beautiful are the feet of those who bring good news of good things!"
—**Romans 10:13-15**

Jesus heard that they had put him out, and finding him, He said, "Do you believe in the Son of Man?"

He answered, "Who is He, Lord, that I may believe in Him?"

Jesus said to him, "You have both seen Him, and He is the one who is talking with you."

And he said, "Lord, I believe." And he worshiped Him.

—John 9:35-38

Another way of stating the first essential component is that faith must have an
(5)   *OBJECT*   . In other words, the object of faith is the something—about which you have knowledge—in which you put your trust. You can't believe in it (have faith) if you don't know about it (have never heard).

Read John 9:35-38 in a Bible or in the margin of this page. (If you are not familiar with this incident of Jesus healing the blind man, you will want to read John 9:1-34 as background for this question.)

What was keeping the blind man from believing in Jesus (as the Son of Man)? (vv. 35-36)   *LACK OF KNOWLEDGE*

What did Jesus do? (v. 37)

What was the result? (v. 38)

Explain briefly how this illustrates the point of the apostle Paul in Romans 10:13-15 above.

(6) True/False. According to the New Testament passages considered above, people can believe in Jesus and be saved even if they have never heard of Him.

Read Acts 4:12 (Peter and John to the Jews), Acts 8:35 (Philip to the eunuch God-fearer), Acts 10:42-43 (Peter to the Gentiles), John 3:16 (John to all) in a Bible. What is the object which all of these proclaimed when calling people to believe or have faith?

Therefore, Christian faith as depicted in the Bible includes knowledge, i.e., knowledge of (7) _____ _____ as its object.

For whom is it intended that Jesus should be the object of their faith? (See Romans 10:11-12.)

Many of Jesus' contemporaries were skeptical about His claims to be God, but eventually moved from unbelief to faith. Using the biblical examples of Thomas (John 20:24-28) and Saul, who became the apostle Paul (Acts 9:1-20), explain briefly how knowledge was an essential component that resulted in a confession of faith.

Following the passage about Thomas, John summarized his reasons for recording in his Gospel the signs (miracles) that Jesus performed in His ministry. Read John 20:30-31 in a Bible or the margin of this page. What purpose did he have?

What did Jesus Himself teach should result from knowledge of His miracles? (See John 10:37-38 and 14:11.)

An important consequence of this truth that faith must have an object is that the validity of your Christian faith is not dependent on how you feel (defeated vs. victorious), whether you have some doubts (lack of confidence), or even the degree of your sincerity, but rather on the genuineness and certainty of the One you are trusting (Jesus Christ).

Read 1 Corinthians 15:13-14 and 17 in a Bible or the margin of this page. What happens to the value and validity of your faith if the claims made about its object, Jesus Christ, are false?

This is also why it was so important in chapters 5 and 6 to establish from the eyewitness historical evidence that Jesus is truly God. Only if this is true can it be concluded that the Christian faith has a (8) _____ object (SBF, pp. 74-75). And only if we have a certain object can our faith be (9) _____.

Furthermore, this knowledge is the basis for choosing Jesus rather than Brahman, Allah, Sai Baba, Maharishi Mehesh Yogi, Nirvana, Sun Myung Moon or any other "god" beckoning to be the object of our faith. We have learned the solid evidential basis supporting Jesus as the genuine article.
Clearly, this understanding of the Christian faith demonstrates that it is not anti-_____! (10) (SBF, p. 75)

(11) True/False. Evidence and reason leading to a greater knowledge about an object are replacements for faith; that is, if you have evidence or knowledge about the object of your faith, you don't need any faith.

The Bible identifies the (12) _____ as a second essential component of faith (SBF, p. 75).

It needs to be made clear that knowledge alone is not faith, and it's possible to

---

Therefore many other signs Jesus also performed in the presence of the disciples, which are not written in this book; but these have been written so that you may believe that Jesus is the Christ, the Son of God; and that believing you may have life in His name.
—John 20:30-31

"If I do not do the works of My Father, do not believe Me; but if I do them, though you do not believe Me, believe the works, so that you may know and understand that the Father is in Me, and I in the Father."
—John 10:37-38

"Believe Me that I am in the Father and the Father is in Me; otherwise believe because of the works themselves."
—John 14:11

But if there is no resurrection of the dead, not even Christ has been raised; and if Christ has not been raised, then our preaching is vain, your faith also is vain... and if Christ has not been raised, your faith is worthless; you are still in your sins.
—1 Corinthians 15:13-14, 17

Essential Component of Faith #2

have knowledge, even of Jesus Christ, without its resulting in any faith. Likewise, an agreeable and consenting will alone is not faith. It is, however, another essential component of the Bible's depiction of faith.

But as for Israel He says, "All the day long I have stretched out my hands to a disobedient and obstinate people."
—**Romans 10:21**

Read Romans 10:21 in a Bible or the margin of this page. Who is Paul talking about here?

Israel wandered forty years in the wilderness because they did not believe or trust that God could take them into the Promised Land. Did Israel have knowledge of God and His promises to them at that time? (See Romans 10:16, 18-19.)

Was their lack of faith, then, due to a lack of knowledge?

How does Paul describe Israel's real problem in verse 21? In other words, why didn't their knowledge result in faith?

The writer of Hebrews comments about this incident in Israel's history. (See Hebrews 3:12-19.) The author's conclusion is that they were not able to enter the Promised Land because of (13) _____ (v. 19). They had a "will" problem, i.e., they refused to believe! In the Scriptures, a rebellious or reluctant will is often equated with a hardened (14) _____ (e.g. Mark 3:5; Ephesians 4:18; Hebrews 3:15).

While under house arrest in Rome, the apostle Paul was given the opportunity to spend all day with Jews "trying to persuade them concerning Jesus." Read about it in Acts 28:23-28.

What two responses did he get?

Concerning those who "would not believe" (v. 24), Paul applied an Old Testament prophecy (vv. 26-27, quoting Isaiah 6:9-10). Does this prophecy attribute a "knowledge" or a "will" reason that they didn't believe (have faith)?

Why will the salvation of God include the Gentiles? (v. 28)

Therefore many of the Jews who came to Mary, and saw what He had done, believed in Him. But some of them went to the Pharisees and told them the things which Jesus had done.
—**John 11:45-46**

Read John 11:45-46 in a Bible or the margin of this page. (If you are not familiar with the event of Jesus raising Lazarus from the dead, read vv. 30-44 as background for this question.) What two responses did Jesus get from those who observed this miracle? (vv. 45-46)

What evil intent did those who did not believe plan? (See vv. 46-48, and 53.)

What essential component of faith does this suggest was keeping them from believing?

[15] True/False. A hardened heart (or reluctant will) can be a component that prevents us from having faith (Hebrews 3:12-13).

Therefore, we conclude that each person must have a consenting will to acknowledge Jesus as Lord and accept His teachings in order to have faith as depicted in the Bible.

The Bible identifies our [16] _____ **as a third essential component of faith** (SBF, p. 77).

Is faith the same as "good intentions" (knowledge of Jesus and agreement with Him)? Read in a Bible or in the margin of this page what Jesus had to say about this (Matthew 21:28-32). Jesus used this parable to illustrate the lack of faith on the part of the Jewish chief priests and elders. Complete the following by filling in the blanks.

The parable of the two sons illustrates the importance of being [17] _____.

The obedience of the one son was demonstrated by his [18] _____.

The tax collectors and prostitutes were going to heaven because they believed, which included acting on John the Baptist's message of the need to repent of their sins (Matthew 3:1-2). The chief priests and elders did not believe—proven by their failure to act upon this message, i.e., they didn't [19] _____.

The point that Jesus is making is that faith is proven by its [20] _____. If there is no action or obedience derived from the will and the knowledge, then there is no evidence of [21] _____ itself.

This is also the point of Jesus' parable of two house builders recorded in Luke 6:46-49. Read it in a Bible or in the SBF text (p. 78). In your own words, identify the essential difference between the two types of people Jesus was illustrating.

Read Matthew 16:24 in a Bible and complete the blanks. Jesus said, "If any one wishes to come after Me, let him deny himself, and take up his cross, and [22]

_____ _____ ."

But some of them went to the Pharisees and told them the things which Jesus had done.

Therefore the chief priests and the Pharisees convened a council, and were saying, "What are we doing? For this man is performing many signs. If we let Him go on like this, all men will believe in Him, and the Romans will come and take away both our place and our nation."
...So from that day on they planned together to kill Him.

—John 11:46-48, 53

Essential Component of Faith #3

"But what do you think? A man had two sons, and he came to the first and said, 'Son, go work today in the vineyard.' And he answered, 'I will not'; but afterward he regretted it and went.

"The man came to the second and said the same thing; and he answered, 'I will, sir'; but he did not go.

"Which of the two did the will of his father?" They said, "The first." Jesus said to them, "Truly I say to you that the tax collectors and prostitutes will get into the kingdom of God before you. For John came to you in the way of righteousness and you did not believe him; but the tax collectors and prostitutes did believe him; and you, seeing this, did not even feel remorse afterward so as to believe him."

—Matthew 21:28-32

(23) Which of the three essential components of faith does the teaching in Matthew 16:24 emphasize?

a) knowledge
b) will
c) response

Does including the third component—that response is essential to the definition of faith—support the argument that good works are necessary in order to earn heaven? Write down what you would say to support a "no" answer to this question.

Our biblical study in this chapter has helped us identify three essential components of faith and another important *FaithSearch* Discovery.

Discovery #7
Certain Object, Valid Faith

Discovery #6
Jesus Backed His Claim

Discovery #5
Jesus Claimed to be God

Discovery #4
Historically Reliable Records

Discovery #3
Eyewitness Records

Discovery #2
God Became Flesh

Discovery #1
No God? DEATH Wins

Ah-ha!
The DISCOVERY

Christian faith is valid because its object, Jesus Christ, is certain!

A legitimate Christian faith is not dependent on us or our circumstances, but on the certainty of its object—Jesus Christ!

Application and Reflection

Which of the three components of faith do you think is most often neglected in the lives of people in the Church? Why do you think this is true?

Jesus said that to follow Him means having a faith that includes obedience to His teaching (John 14:15; Luke 14:27). He speaks of the reality of demons and of the devil as our tempter and enemy. In view of the teaching in this chapter about faith being valid because it is based on a certain object (Jesus Christ) write a brief answer to someone who asks how you are being reasonable to believe in such things as demons and a devil. Read the discussion below for further insight.

Disputing the Existence of Demons

Are the New Testament accounts of demons true?

The New Testament, including Jesus Himself, clearly teaches the existence of a spiritual realm of demonic and angelic personal beings. The former are evil (sinning and rebelling from their created state as angels) and the latter are obedient servants of God. Some people today dismiss such beings as a pre-scientific way of describing psychological dysfunctions such as hysteria or epilepsy. While it is true that at certain times in history some sects of Christianity have abused people with this doctrine of demons, it is primarily because of the actions and teachings of Jesus about nonphysical beings that we are capable of avoiding such abuse and having a more complete understanding of the universe.

The New Testament refers to angels 176 times, to Satan (or the devil) 65 times, and demons or unclean spirits 75 times. See Matthew 1:20; 2:13; 4:1-11; 8:28-34; 9:32-35; and John 8:44 for examples. In view of the New Testament's teaching, to deny the possibility of the existence of angels and demons would, by extension, lead to the rejection of all spiritual beings, including God.

Some forms of physical disease and dysfunction are attributed to demons in the Gospels, including incidents of paralysis (Luke 13:10-13), violence and bodily mutilation (Mark 5:1-20) and epilepsy (Matthew 17:14-18). But it should be noted that not all diseases are associated with demons, because the New Testament differentiates between healing diseases and casting out demons. Therefore, we need to take a balanced perspective, neither denying that personal evil spirits exist nor seeing them "behind every bush." If they are encountered, the believer in Christ will find sufficient power in Him to expel them.

There is a logical explanation as to why the devil and demonic beings seemed to be particularly active at the time of Jesus. He came with the power of the Kingdom of God to set individuals free from sin and remove them from the devil's kingdom of darkness. We would expect such spiritual salvation to be met with opposition.

> Thus the demons are part of the cosmic or spiritual conflict going on behind the outward actions [by Jesus] of preaching, teaching and healing. Demons fit into the New Testament picture of what the reign of God means and the fact that salvation is not simply deliverance from physical sickness or political oppression or poverty, but at root a deliverance from final judgment, from spiritual sin and from the oppression by evil spiritual forces connected to these things" (Walter Kaiser, Jr., et. al., *Hard Sayings of the Bible* [InterVarsity, 1997]).

Read and reflect on John 6:66-69. You may have had times of hardship, discouragement or confusion in your Christian life as faced by the disciples of Jesus here. At times like that in the past, were you ever tempted to "toss in the towel" because your faith didn't seem real, because it didn't "work," or because you didn't feel you could keep it up? Describe your response briefly.

As a result of this many of His disciples withdrew and were not walking with Him anymore. So Jesus said to the twelve, "You do not want to go away also, do you?"

Simon Peter answered Him, "Lord, to whom shall we go? You have words of eternal life. We have believed and have come to know that You are the Holy One of God."

—**John 6:66-69**

How can what you have learned about faith in this chapter help you at times like that in the future? Is your faith any less certain because you feel weak or even because you may have failed? Has the object of your faith (Jesus) changed? Write down your thoughts and some ideas for a new plan of action for your future response in your Christian walk.

FaithSearch Discovery demonstrates that the Christian faith is reasonable. But suppose a friend said to you, "If I had reasons, I wouldn't need faith." How would you answer?

The three essential components of a biblically valid faith can be summed up in this faith definition (SBF, pp. 79-80): "Faith is a [24] _____- _____ _____, based upon a certain object, and without regard to any emotional questioning of that object."

Faith as a "commitment-making process" involves knowing, willing and responding. Think this process through as you apply it to starting a fast-food restaurant, by answering the following:

What would you do first to determine if the restaurant is a good idea?

If you are certain that it is a good idea, what must you do next in order to get the project started?

Having built a fast-food restaurant, what must you do in the last step of the process that is necessary to bring your idea to reality, i.e., serving burgers, fries and malts?

Write down some of your thoughts about the parallels you see between this process and helping someone move from unbelief to faith in Jesus Christ.

Understanding the essential components of faith is helpful to making us more effective witnesses because it also helps us discern the true cause of someone's unbelief. Read pages 92-94 in SBF and match the description on the right with the form of unbelief on the left (below). [25]

_____Ignorant unbelief   a. willful, hard-hearted, rejection, rebellion

_____Doubt   b. unknowing, blind

_____Decisional unbelief   c. skepticism, distrust, wavering, indecision

Read pages 94-96 in SBF and refer to the diagram on page 101. What must a person in each of the forms of unbelief above do to get out of that condition?

Ignorant unbelief:

It is essential that those who already have faith in Jesus are active in telling unbelievers about Him and supporting those who have been called of God to do this full time. Only if we (26) _Tell_ others is it possible for unbelievers to understand who Jesus is and confess Him as the object of their faith.

Doubt:

It is essential that those who already have faith in Jesus give assurance to those who are wavering that Jesus, if confessed as their Savior and Lord, will never leave them or forsake them.

Decisional unbelief:

It is essential that those who already have faith in Jesus are active in (27) _____ for unbelievers who have rejected the Good News of new life in Jesus. Only God can turn a hardened heart back to a reconsideration of the evidence and a faith commitment to Himself.

Confirming the Discovery

Read the references below in a Bible, or as provided here in the margin. Write after each one how it relates to or confirms the discovery made in this chapter.

Romans 10:17

Ephesians 4:18   separated because of ignorance

1 Timothy 2:5

Hebrews 2:3-4   ignore salvation -

Philippians 2:9-11   Jesus elevated

Luke 24:46-48

So then, faith comes from hearing the message, and the message comes through preaching Christ.
        —Romans 10:17 (TEV)

They are darkened in their understanding and separated from the life of God because of the ignorance that is in them due to the hardening of their hearts.
        —Ephesians 4:18 (NIV)

For there is one God, and one mediator also between God and men, the man Christ Jesus…
        —1 Timothy 2:5

…how will we escape if we neglect so great a salvation? After it was at the first spoken through the Lord, it was confirmed to us by those who heard, God also testifying with them, both by signs and wonders and by various miracles and by gifts of the Holy Spirit according to His own will.
        —Hebrews 2:3-4

For this reason also, God highly exalted Him, and bestowed on Him the name which is above every name, so that at the name of Jesus every knee will bow, of those who are in heaven, and on earth, and under the earth, and that every tongue will confess that Jesus Christ is Lord, to the glory of God the Father.
        —Philippians 2:9-11

[A]nd He said to them, "Thus it is written, that the Christ should suffer and rise again from the dead the third day; and that repentance for forgiveness of sins should be proclaimed in His name to all the nations…. You are witnesses of these things."
        —Luke 24:46-48

In summary of God's Word, we discovered that faith must have an object and that object is Jesus Christ (Romans 10:17). People who are either ignorant of that fact or have hardened their hearts to that truth are separated from God (Ephesians 4:18), for Jesus is the only one who can bring God and people together (1 Timothy 2:5).

God made His salvation perfectly clear through the Lord's own words which were confirmed by His eyewitness disciples. But even more convincing was God's authentication through miracles and through spiritual gifts bestowed by the Holy Spirit (Hebrews 2:3-4).

As a result of Jesus' sacrificial death and resurrection, He has been exalted to the highest authority in the universe and all will ultimately acknowledge and confess His Lordship (Philippians 2:9-11). Until then, we who believe are to be witnesses, proclaiming that in Jesus' name there is forgiveness of sin (Luke 24:46-48).

Looking Ahead

If what you have learned in this chapter has left you feeling a little uneasy about the nature of faith, or you have a desire for something more, that's good. You should be uneasy—and there is more! Something very important is indeed missing. In the next chapter we'll discover what that is. We'll also discover the life-changing dimensions of faith which result when we embrace Jesus Christ as Savior and Lord.

Answers for the objective questions in this chapter:

1. noun	2. verb	3. knowledge	4. I believe in SOMETHING
5. object	6. False	7. Jesus Christ	8. certain
9. valid	10. intellectual	11. False	12. will
13. unbelief	14. heart	15. True	16. response
17. obedient	18. action	19. repent	20. response
21. faith	22. follow Me	23. c	24. commitment-making process
25. Ignorant unbelief = b, Doubt = c, Decisional unbelief = a			
26. tell	27. prayer		

CHAPTER 8

A Miracle of New Life from Above
Discovering the Life-Changing Dimensions of Faith

Getting FOCUSED

- Is Christian faith essentially adhering to a code of ethics that prescribes moral behavior?
- What if I become a Christian but can't keep up the lifestyle?
- Are there objective and observable results of Christian faith that I should experience in my life?

The Christian faith is often viewed as just another religious ethical system to regulate behavior. It is often thought that to become a Christian means "turning over a new leaf," "cleaning up your act," or "getting religion." This same thinking identifies "becoming a Christian" only with conforming to a prescribed lifestyle. These are serious misunderstandings. The Christian faith begins with a miracle in our life—resulting in a personal relationship with God. It also sets us free from performance in order to please God, and gives us a new hope—the assurance of eternal life in heaven.

Making the DISCOVERY

The text of *FaithSearch* Discovery, *Surprised by Faith* (pp. 83-89) will help you to answer the questions and make the discovery in this chapter.

Introduction

I am certain that the three components of faith identified in the last chapter are consistent with New Testament teaching. But if that were all the New Testament taught about faith, it would be possible to draw a false conclusion. We may naively think that we could follow Jesus and His teachings in the flesh, using our own goodness, discipline, and determination. What does the Bible say about this?

Something Wrong – Something Missing

The Human Problem

The Bible is clear that the reason we cannot follow Jesus and His teachings is a problem in our own nature. We have neither the desire nor the capability to follow Him.

Read Mark 7:20-23 in a Bible or the margin of this page. Where does Jesus say that evil thoughts and deeds come from?

A Leader's Guide is available with answers to these questions, guidelines for leading small group interaction, and other helpful resources. It's available free by downloading it from the *FaithSearch* Web site (www.faithsearch.org). For a small fee plus postage, a printed copy can be requested from the *FaithSearch* office (952-401-4501).

He went on: "What comes out of a man is what makes him 'unclean.' For from within, out of men's hearts, come evil thoughts, sexual immorality, theft, murder, adultery, greed, malice, deceit, lewdness, envy, slander, arrogance and folly. All these evils come from inside and make a man 'unclean.'"
*—**Mark 7:20-23 (NIV)***

The LORD smelled the pleasing aroma and said in his heart: "Never again will I curse the ground because of man, even though every inclination of his heart is evil from childhood. And never again will I destroy all living creatures, as I have done."
—Genesis 8:21 (NIV)

The heart is deceitful above all things and beyond cure. Who can understand it?
—Jeremiah 17:9 (NIV)

"You have heard that it was said, 'Do not commit adultery.' But I tell you that anyone who looks at a woman lustfully has already committed adultery with her in his heart."
—Matthew 5:27-28 (NIV)

"…But I tell you: Love your enemies and pray for those who persecute you,…"
—Matthew 5:44 (NIV)

"Be perfect, therefore, as your heavenly Father is perfect."
—Matthew 5:48 (NIV)

Then Peter came to Jesus and asked, "Lord, how many times shall I forgive my brother when he sins against me? Up to seven times?" Jesus answered, "I tell you, not seven times, but seventy-seven times."
—Matthew 18:21-22 (NIV)

"In the same way, any of you who does not give up everything he has cannot be my disciple."
—Luke 14:33 (NIV)

Read also Genesis 8:21 and Jeremiah 17:9. What is the condition of the heart (i.e. the nature) of each one of us?

In your own words, summarize briefly the spiritual nature of man based on these Old Testament statements together with the teaching of Jesus above?

We may deny that our natural condition is so corrupt or fallen, arguing that we are not *that* bad. But we need to ask what we would think and do if there were no restraints or consequences to our actions—if no one ever knew or found out.

There is yet another problem: We have each personally experienced our own moral ineptness in measuring up to the high standard of Jesus' teachings. To illustrate this, read the following passages and write what Jesus says is expected of us.

Matthew 5:27-28

Matthew 5:44

Matthew 5:48

Matthew 18:21-22

Luke 14:33

In view of this high standard, it is tempting to throw up our arms in despair. Even our thoughts and motives are declared to be sin! The apostle Paul wrestled with this same problem. Read Romans 7:14-25 in your Bible and answer the following questions.

What does he acknowledge is the nature of his "flesh"?

Does he have the power to free himself from his sin nature?

How did he finally find freedom from sin and guilt before God?

The most common offense expressed against Christianity is that a good God would never keep good people out of heaven, and certainly would not send them to hell! Aren't good people good enough? This legitimate concern reflects the greatest misunderstanding people have about the Christian faith: that it is a system of works by which we earn a place in heaven. How would you answer someone with this view? Read the following discussion for assistance in formulating your answer. (Write in the margin as needed.)

Aren't Good People Good Enough?

Take, for example, an atheist who is a good citizen, kind to people and gives to charity: Would he/she still go to hell and be separated from God forever?

Everyone who contemplates that someone would be separated from God and spend eternity in hell ought to do so with tears in their eyes. It is not a thought that a Christian can enjoy or feel smug about. Emotionally, everyone wants to believe that a loving God would place everyone in heaven. However, our feelings are usually quite subjective and are not the way to arrive at objective truth. What are the biblical facts?

God, as revealed in the Bible, loves people so much that He has provided a way for all to be in heaven! According to Jesus, a person goes to hell because of his/her personal sin, such as independence from God and moral failure (John 8:24, 34). To have all people in heaven and out of hell, there must be a way to remove the sin that separates each and every one of us from God (Isaiah 59:2). God is willing to forgive, but cannot violate His holy and just character by doing so unjustly. That is, a righteous God cannot ignore or "wink" sin away. There must be an appropriate ransom or redemption offered that meets the just requirements of the law of God so that in love He can forgive us without Himself becoming unjust in doing so.

Because all humans are sinners, they are incapable of offering to God the righteous ransom needed to redeem humanity, i.e., to make forgiveness possible for them. As recorded in Psalm 49:7, "No man can by any means redeem his brother, or give to God a ransom for him…" Every religion must address and resolve this dilemma. Nearly all do so by encouraging us to do good deeds that offset the sin. The argument is that if our good works exceed our personal sins, then on the basis of merit we have earned a place in heaven. This approach ignores God's perfect holiness and justice, and assumes God will compromise both standards if we make a sincere effort. God can't do that without becoming immoral, i.e., violating His character and thereby ceasing to be an absolutely holy and just God.

Instead, "…God so loved the world, that He gave His only begotten Son, that whoever believes in Him shall not perish, but have eternal life" (John 3:16). God became incarnate on earth as Jesus, the Son of God, who offered His sinless life on the cross as the ultimate and worthy ransom, which satisfied the just character of God (Mark 10:45). Jesus' death was a substitute—He took the death we each deserve and offered eternal life to us in exchange (1 Peter 3:18). As a result, God forgives all our sin and declares that we are holy (no longer under sin's condemnation—Romans 8:1). It's free (i.e., to us—but it cost Jesus His life!) and is offered to us through God's love and grace.

Of course, we must embrace Jesus Christ as the resurrected Lord by a personal response of repentance and confession of faith (Romans 10:9). This is the Gospel of Good News which Jesus asked His followers to proclaim to all peoples everywhere (Luke 24:46-48; Matthew 28:18-20). Whether in person or by various forms of media, Christian proclamation of this Good News is now global. Therefore, for most people of the world, the dilemma is not a God who sends people to hell, but their ignorance of, or hardness toward, the true and freely-offered way to heaven. There is a cure for the disease called sin, but you have to be aware of–and willing to take–the medicine!

For more information, see "Is It Your Fault You've Never Heard Of Jesus?" (p. 83 below), and these books:

Lee Strobel, *The Case for Faith* (Grand Rapids: Zondervan Publishing, 2000), pp. 169-194.

Ronald Nash, *Is Jesus the Only Savior?* (Grand Rapids: Zondervan Publishing, 1994).

Donald Bierle, *Making Sense of Creation and Evolution* (**FaithSearch** International, 2001), chapter 7.

Jesus answered and said to him, "Truly, truly, I say to you, unless one is born again he cannot see the kingdom of God."

Nicodemus said to Him, "How can a man be born when he is old? He cannot enter a second time into his mother's womb and be born, can he?"

Jesus answered, "Truly, truly, I say to you, unless one is born of water and the Spirit he cannot enter into the kingdom of God. That which is born of the flesh is flesh, and that which is born of the Spirit is spirit."

—John 3:3-6

God's Solution to the Human Problem

Read John 3:3-6 in a Bible or the margin of this page (SBF, pp. 84-85).

Who is Jesus talking to here?

Was Nicodemus quite religious and spiritually respected as righteous by Jewish people of that day?

What did Jesus say that Nicodemus lacked to go to heaven (i.e. the Kingdom of God)?

What words does Jesus use to describe this in v. 6?

Jesus told this religious leader Nicodemus, one of the seventy on the highest court in the land (the Sanhedrin) and respected for his righteous adherence to the Law, that he wasn't going to heaven! Why?

The Greek original from which we translate "born again" literally means to have [1] *new* *life* *from* *above* (SBF, p. 84)—one is spiritually and miraculously conceived by the Holy Spirit to become a child of God. This concept is a consistent teaching of the New Testament. Confirm this by reading each passage below in your Bible, then match it with the description on the left. [2]

b Born again to a living hope   a. 1 John 5:1

a Whoever believes that Jesus is the Christ is born of God   b. 1 Peter 1:3

d Born not…of the will of man, but of God   c. 1 John 3:9

e Born again…through the living and abiding word of God   d. John 1:13

c No one who is born of God practices sin   e. 1 Peter 1:23

Therefore, faith as taught in the Bible not only has the three essential components discussed in the last chapter, but also has this all-important [3] *Supernatural* component. Becoming a Christian requires a [4] *MIRACLE* of God! This is what was missing from our faith discussion in the last chapter (SBF, pp. 86-87).

Use the words below to label the triangle in the margin of this page so it reflects a more complete understanding of the nature of biblical faith.

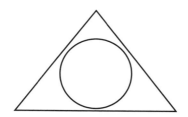

Knowledge of Jesus Christ

Will to confess Jesus as Lord

Response to follow Jesus in obedience

Holy Spirit to create in us a miraculous new life from above

Read Romans 8:9 in a Bible or the margin of this page. According to the apostle Paul, how serious is it if we don't have the Holy Spirit within us?

However, you are not in the flesh but in the Spirit, if indeed the Spirit of God dwells in you. But if anyone does not have the Spirit of Christ, he does not belong to Him.
—Romans 8:9

Once again, consider why each of us needs forgiveness and the miracle of new life. Match the passage on the right with the problem identified on the left. [5]

_____Our sin has separated us from God   a. Romans 3:22b-23

_____We are in bondage to our sin   b. Romans 5:12 and 6:23

_____Our lives have fallen short of God's glory c. Isaiah 59:2

_____Because of sin, our destiny is death   d. John 8:34

[6] True/False. According to the Bible, the way to become a Christian is, so to speak, "turning over a new leaf" in our life—to stop using profanity, clean up impure thoughts, go to church once a week, try to be kind and generous, and pray before meals.

Based on the teaching so far in this chapter, prepare a brief answer to someone who says to you that they are a Christian and going to heaven because they have tried to live a good life. (See Ephesians 2:8-9.)

Three Life-Changing Dimensions of Faith

Becoming a Christian establishes you in a new [7] _____ **with God** (SBF, p. 83).

During His ministry, Jesus taught that a supernatural event would occur in His disciples' lives. Read John 7:37-39 in a Bible or the margin of this page.

Jesus' references to being "thirsty" and coming to Him to "drink" are metaphors for what?

Life-Changing Dimension #1

Now on the last day, the great day of the feast, Jesus stood and cried out, saying, "If anyone is thirsty, let him come to Me and drink. He who believes in Me, as the Scripture said, 'From his innermost being will flow rivers of living water.'" But this He spoke of the Spirit, whom those who believed in Him were to receive; for the Spirit was not yet given, because Jesus was not yet glorified.
—John 7:37-39

"I will ask the Father, and He will give you another Helper, that He may be with you forever; that is the Spirit of truth, whom the world cannot receive, because it does not see Him or know Him, but you know Him because He abides with you and will be in you."
—John 14:16-17

Therefore, if anyone is in Christ, he is a new creation; the old has gone, the new has come!
—2 Corinthians 5:17 (NIV)

But as many as received Him, to them He gave the right to become children of God, even to those who believe in His name...
—John 1:12

Life-Changing Dimension #2

From where will the "streams of living water" flow?

Who does Jesus say will receive the Holy Spirit?

This supernatural event of receiving the Holy Spirit results in a special relationship with God for Jesus' followers now that He is no longer physically present on the earth. Read John 14:16-17 in a Bible or the margin of this page.

What did Jesus say He would request from the Father for His followers?

Jesus refers to this new Helper as the [8] _____ of truth (v. 17).

Where will this new Helper (i.e. Comforter; Counselor; Advocate) reside? (Confirm your answer by reading 1 Corinthians 6:19 and 2 Corinthians 1:22.)

[9] True/False. When we make a confession of faith in Jesus, we experience a new relationship, the gift of God's presence—the Holy Spirit—within us.

As a result of this supernatural event of receiving the Holy Spirit, we become a new creation and are adopted into the family of God.

Read 2 Corinthians 5:17 in a Bible or the margin of this page. Everyone who has professed Christ as Lord is a new [10] _____. The [11] _____ is gone, the [12] _____ has come.

Read John 1:12 in a Bible or the margin of this page. All who have professed Christ as Lord have become [13] _____ of God.

Where does the assurance that we are children of God come from? (See Romans 8:16.)

Two personal beings, God and you, at one time alienated by sin, are now reconciled by the substitutionary sacrifice of Jesus. As a result you have the [14] _____ of your sin, God lives [15] _____ you, and you have become a [16] _____ of God. You are family!

Becoming a Christian releases you from the treadmill of performance and fear into a new [17] *FREEDOM* (SBF, p. 85).

Salvation in most other religions of the world is based on personal merit. Of course, no one in those religions really knows how many deeds are enough to earn the goal. They are left to try even harder and must live with uncertainty and fear. Christianity as taught in the Bible is not like that.

Bertrand Russell, a twentieth century British mathematician and philosopher, and critic of Christianity, said, "The Christian principle 'Love your enemies' is good...except that it is too difficult for most of us..." (*A History of Western Philosophy*, [New York: Simon and Schuster, 1972], p. 602).

C.S. Lewis, scholar and noted Christian author and apologist, agreed when he wrote, "Every one says forgiveness is a lovely idea, until they have something to forgive..." (*Mere Christianity*, [New York: The Macmillan Company, 1960], p. 104).

Read Romans 8:6-8 in a Bible or the margin of this page. Identify three truths that are taught there by completing the blanks below.

The "flesh" (human nature and endeavor) is [18] _____ toward God.

The "flesh" is [19] _____ to submit to the ways of God.

No one can [20] _____ God "in the flesh."

Read Romans 8:1-4 in a Bible or the margin of this page, and answer the following questions.

What no longer exists for the believer because of Jesus Christ? (v. 1)

What replaced the Law, sin and the flesh in our lives? (vv. 2-3)

How do we now fulfill the Law and please God? (v. 4)

Read Philippians 2:13 in a Bible or the margin of this page. When we have the Holy Spirit within and live our lives in a way that is pleasing to God, who should be recognized as the source and receive the praise?

[21] True/False. One of the ways that Christianity differs from other religions is that salvation is by forgiveness through God's grace (a gift), rather than by personal merit earned through good deeds (Ephesians 2:8-9).

Becoming a Christian provides you with a new [22] _____ **for life now and forever** (SBF, p. 87).

According to 1 John 5:11-13, who has eternal life?

Why did the apostle John write this letter to believers? (v. 13)

For the mind set on the flesh is death, but the mind set on the Spirit is life and peace, because the mind set on the flesh is hostile toward God; for it does not subject itself to the law of God, for it is not even able to do so, and those who are in the flesh cannot please God.
—**Romans 8:6-8**

"Therefore there is now no condemnation for those who are in Christ Jesus. For the law of the Spirit of life in Christ Jesus has set you free from the law of sin and of death. For what the Law could not do, weak as it was through the flesh, God did: sending His own Son in the likeness of sinful flesh and as an offering for sin, He condemned sin in the flesh, so that the requirement of the Law might be fulfilled in us, who do not walk according to the flesh but according to the Spirit."
—**Romans 8:1-4**

...for it is God who is at work in you, both to will and to work for His good pleasure.
—**Philippians 2:13**

Life-Changing Dimension

#3

In the upper room, the night before His arrest and crucifixion, Jesus talked to the apostles (John 14:1-3).

What did Jesus assure them about space availability in God's heavenly home? (v. 1) *MANY ROOMS*

What two things did Jesus say He would do? (vv. 2-3)

Prepare A Place

I'm coming Back

What wonderful promise did He make to them? (v. 3)

I'll take you with me

(23) True/False. In Christianity, there is certainty of going to heaven. This is because of our new freedom that enables us to earn it by being good.

Note some of the promises in the New Testament about the basis and assurance of eternal life by matching the verse on the right with the truth on the left. (24)

d "…whoever believes in Him shall not perish…"   a. 1 John 2:25 (NIV)

c "…the free gift of God is eternal life in Christ
Jesus our Lord."   b. John 6:40

a "And this is what He promised us—even eternal life." c. Romans 6:23

b "…every one who…believes in Him, will have
eternal life…"   d. John 3:16

Use the Bible passage below to summarize what you have learned. Complete the blanks with the appropriate life-changing dimension of faith.

> "But when the kindness of God our Savior and His love for mankind appeared,
> He saved us, not on the basis of deeds which we have done in righteousness, but
> according to His mercy (our new (25) *FREEDOM*   ), by the washing
> of regeneration and renewing by the Holy spirit, whom He poured out upon us
> richly through Jesus Christ our Savior (our new (26) *RELATIONSHIP*   ),
> that being justified by His grace we might be made heirs according to the hope of
> eternal life (our new (27) *HOPE*   )."
>   —Titus 3:4-7

This is our eighth *FaithSearch* discovery—and what a wonderful discovery it is!

Ah-ha!
The DISCOVERY

Becoming a Christian is a MIRACLE of new life by the Holy Spirit resulting in a new relationship, freedom, and hope!

Application and Reflection

Three life-changing dimensions of the Christian faith were identified in this chapter:

a.   A new relationship with God (the Holy Spirit within)

b.   A new freedom from performance and fear (forgiveness by grace, and power over sin)

c.   A new hope of eternal life (assurance of heaven)

Write your thoughts and evaluation of how these life-changing dimensions of becoming a Christian are the same as, and how they are different from, your previous understanding. How do you respond to them? Are you: excited? skeptical? accepting? cautious?

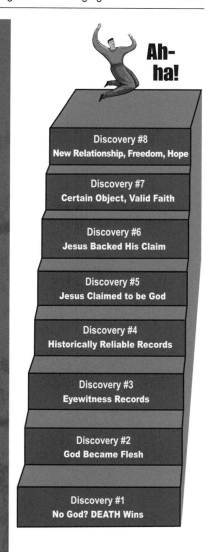

Ah-ha!

Discovery #8
New Relationship, Freedom, Hope

Discovery #7
Certain Object, Valid Faith

Discovery #6
Jesus Backed His Claim

Discovery #5
Jesus Claimed to be God

Discovery #4
Historically Reliable Records

Discovery #3
Eyewitness Records

Discovery #2
God Became Flesh

Discovery #1
No God? DEATH Wins

Most of us have had the experience of hearing someone state that the life changes claimed by Christians are not convincing to them of the truth of their faith. Instead, they maintain that Christians are all hypocrites and they don't want to become like them. How would you answer this? Use the discussion below for help in formulating your answer.

First, the Christian faith is not invalidated by the actions of some Christians in history–or by how they may act today. The truth of Christianity stands or falls on the genuineness of the person of Jesus Christ, which we have demonstrated in the first seven chapters of *FaithSearch* Discovery. Since *He* was not a hypocrite, we are not excused from becoming His follower just because we can find someone whose behavior is inconsistent or turns us off.

Furthermore, you are to be commended for not wanting to be a hypocrite. That's the sin which greatly offended Jesus as well. He said, "Woe to you scribes and Pharisees, hypocrites!" (Matthew 23:23-33). Hypocrisy is pretending to be what we aren't—a sham, phony, often parading a superficial superiority. That's what Jesus condemned. But we must not confuse hypocrisy with personal failure or sin. All Christians (and non-Christians) are sinners, but not all Christians are hypocrites. Often the person who is judging all Christians as hypocrites thinks that what someone means by claiming to be a Christian is that they are better than others. That is a misconception imposed on the Christian they are judging. Becoming a Christian includes admitting you are a sinner and experiencing a forgiveness you do not deserve. (It's a gift given freely by grace, and is not–nor can it be–earned.) Because this is such a meaningful experience, Christians often express openly how this has given them a sense of acceptance, relief and life change. To the non-Christian, this may sound like a "boast" of moral purity and superiority—even judgment on them. Not so. Even though forgiven and changed, Christians may still fail or sin. (In fact, God points out that if we say we do not sin, that we are making Him out to be a liar! See 1 John 1:10.) Clearly, that doesn't mean they are phonies—unless the observer imposes the expectation that the Christian should now be "perfect."

Finally, we cannot implicate all Christians as hypocrites because one or a few in our experience have been. Deceptively corrupt people have been revealed from every walk of life and vocation, whether teacher, salesman, farmer, lawyer, etc. When that person is exposed, do we condemn and reject all education, marketing, agriculture and the legal profession? No, we recognize that one bad apple doesn't mean that they are all rotten, especially when the evidence shows otherwise. Likewise, because it is demonstrated that someone who claims to be Christian may be playing a phony game with his/her alleged faith, this doesn't necessarily mean that all Christians are hypocrites, nor that Christianity is false. Besides, no one can entirely escape the charge of "hypocrite"—no one, that is, except Jesus Himself. And it is only by trusting in Him and experiencing the humility of forgiveness and the security of His love that we are freed to take off our masks and to become "real" people—honest, transparent, and genuine.

Based on what you have learned in this chapter, circle which image below best represents what happens when we **become** a Christian? [28]

    a)   Remodeling an old house (reformation), or

    b)   Metamorphosis of a caterpillar into a butterfly (transformation)

Is **becoming** a Christian more of a reformation or a transformation? Explain your answer. (See John 3:3; Romans 6:4-6; 2 Corinthians 5:17; and Galatians 6:15.)

How about **being** a Christian? Is this more of a reformation or a transformation? Explain your answer. (See 2 Corinthians 3:18; Philippians 1:6; 3:12-15.)

Becoming and **being** are two distinct aspects of the spirituality of a Christian. First, transformation is a thoroughgoing or fundamental change in your spiritual condition, nature, substance and state, a metamorphosis. This is [29] _Becoming_ a Christian. Second, having become a Christian, you are to change—a process of spiritual improvement whereby the Holy Spirit removes faults and adds positive qualities. This is [30] _BEING_ a Christian.

A common question and concern by Christians and non-Christians alike is the fate of those in the world who die without hearing about forgiveness in Jesus Christ. Is it their fault that they never had an opportunity to hear about the cure for sin? What would you say to someone who asked you this? Read the discussion below for help in formulating your answer.

"Is It Your Fault You've Never Heard Of Jesus?"

No one will go to hell because they have never heard of Jesus. People go to hell because the sin in their life separates them from God. Similarly, people do not die because they have never heard of the cure for a disease. They die from the causative agents of the disease, such as a virus or bacteria or genetic defect. This is not an attempt to be evasive or facetious—it is critical to understanding this issue. In the case of spiritual death the causative agent is sin. Is there a cure? Yes, God has already made it available completely free through the substitutionary and atoning death of Jesus Christ, and our embracing that cure through a confession of faith.

What about those who have no opportunity to hear of the cure? There are two important points that are relevant to them. One, God says through the writer of Hebrews that "He is a rewarder of those who seek Him" (Hebrews 11:6b). God knows the seeking heart which is not content with worshipping stones, ancestors, false gods or nothing. He is not locked out of the universe that He created, so He can guide the seeker to a source of the Gospel cure, or bring a messenger of that cure to the seeker. He can even reveal Himself to them in unusual ways to satisfy their spiritually hungry heart. This is not theoretical—it is the actual testimony of many who have been there.

Second, there is a tremendous burden upon each person to realize that their personal sin is not always a private issue. The drunk who crosses into oncoming traffic with his car and kills a family of four is no longer sinning privately. And the four—did they deserve such a fate? Likewise, when a father or mother chooses to live without God, their children often grow up without the opportunity to know God. If that particular father was the founder of a tribe of people, the whole tribe in a sense become victims of the father's sin. God respects our wills and honors our choices, even when the consequences impact others temporally and even eternally.

Because all people in the world today are derived from Noah and his family (who knew and trusted God), then it follows that somewhere along the genealogies since then, there were some who broke the chain of faith through their sin—and ignorance and deception concerning God was the result for their descendents. They are lost because of sin—whether no one has told them about the cure or they have denied it. That's why Jesus was so insistent and passionate about His command that "…repentance for forgiveness of sins would be proclaimed in His name to all the nations…" (Luke 24:47). He wept over lost Jerusalem (Luke 19:41-44) and said He came to seek and to save the lost in the world (Luke 19:10). We who have experienced the cure need to shout the Good News to others from the housetops!

The *worst* thing you can do if you are truly concerned about those who are outside the influence of the Christian faith (i.e. those who have never heard), is

For more details on this subject, see: John Sanders, ed., *What About Those Who Have Never Heard?* (Downers Grove: InterVarsity Press, 1995).

Lee Strobel, *The Case for Faith* (Grand Rapids: Zondervan Publishing, 2000), pp. 145-167 and 223-245.

For whatever is born of God overcomes the world; and this is the victory that has overcome the world—our faith.

—**1 John 5:4**

For by grace you have been saved through faith; and that not of yourselves, it is the gift of God; not as a result of works, that no one may boast.

—**Ephesians 2:8-9**

Because you are sons, God has sent forth the Spirit of His Son into our hearts, crying, 'Abba! Father!'

Therefore, you are no longer a slave, but a son; and if a son, then an heir through God.

—**Galatians 4:6-7**

...for it is God who works in you to will and act according to His good purpose.

—**Philippians 2:13 (NIV)**

"Let your light shine before men in such a way that they may see your good works, and glorify your Father who is in heaven."

—**Matthew 5:16**

for yourself to *remain* outside. You aren't helping by being critical of the problem or denying that a problem exists. Help proclaim the cure!

Children, the mentally challenged, etc. are considered by most Christians to be special cases, and not to be destined for hell. For more insight on this and other relevant questions, see the books in the margin.

Confirming the Discovery

Read the references below in a Bible, or as provided here in the margin. Write after each one how the main teaching of each relates to or confirms the discovery made in this chapter.

1 John 5:4

Ephesians 2:8-9

Galatians 4:6-7

Philippians 2:13

Matthew 5:16

In summary of God's Word, God does a miracle in our lives when we confess faith in Jesus, and sets us free from our bondage to sin and death (1 John 5:4). Grace and forgiveness are necessary because we are morally and spiritually bankrupt before a holy God. As a gift, salvation cannot be earned by any good deeds we do (Ephesians 2:8-9).

As a result, we have a personal relationship with God because we are created anew by the Holy Spirit who indwells us. We are adopted into His very family as His children (Galatians 4:6-7). Having the Holy Spirit within us means that we please God because God Himself is transforming our lives by inspiring our wills and empowering our response to obey His word (Philippians 2:13). These life changes which God causes in us are a testimony to the unbeliever. Unbelievers are drawn to our heavenly Father because of the integrity and holiness they observe in us (Matthew 5:16).

Looking Ahead

Are you willing to give God permission to miraculously transform you into a new person, and reform you more and more into the image of the Lord Jesus Christ? Hopefully and prayerfully your answer is "YES!"

But sometimes there can be a hesitancy or reluctance in our spirit to the changes God wants to make in our life. In fact, the Bible identifies one particular factor that keeps more people from faith and the growth of faith than any other. What is this stumbling block to faith? We'll discover that in the next chapter.

Answers for the objective questions in this chapter:

1. new life from above   2. b, a, d, e, c   3. supernatural   4. miracle
5. c, d, a, b   6. False   7. relationship   8. Spirit
9. True   10. creation   11. old   12. new
13. children   14. forgiveness   15. within   16. child
17. freedom   18. hostile   19. unable   20. please
21. True   22. hope   23. False   24. d, c, a, b
25. freedom   26. relationship   27. hope   28. b
29. becoming   30. being

CHAPTER 9

How Can I Know God?
Discovering the Stumbling Block
Along the Path to Faith

Getting FOCUSED

- What is the greatest deterrent that keeps people from faith and a relationship with God?

- What two key questions must everyone ask and honestly answer along their path to faith?

- What is the principle of "spiritual brokenness"?

A Leader's Guide is available with answers to these questions, guidelines for leading small group interaction, and other helpful resources. It's available free by downloading it from the *FaithSearch* Web site (www.faithsearch.org). For a small fee plus postage, a printed copy can be requested from the *FaithSearch* office (952-401-4501).

We have discovered evidence which can satisfy the mind concerning the certainty of the object of faith, Jesus Christ. Yet there is a powerful factor which may make us reluctant to take the next step along the path to faith. In fact, it is often the primary reason that some people find Christianity hard, and never come to know God or experience the life-transforming dimensions of faith. Honestly answering two key questions can lead to a biblical principle called "spiritual brokenness"—which is often the antidote to this menacing stumbling block. This is the discovery we will make in this chapter.

Making the DISCOVERY

The text of *FaithSearch* Discovery, *Surprised by Faith* (pp. 105-117) will help you to answer the questions and make the discovery in this chapter.

Introduction

During His ministry, Jesus told a parable about a nobleman who went away to receive a kingdom and become a king (Luke 19:12-27). He gave his servants money to carry on his business while he was gone. In the meantime his citizenry rebelled and sent a message: "We do not want this man to reign over us." Eventually the nobleman returned with authority as king, rewarded his servants who had been good stewards, and executed those who had rejected him. The parable was applicable to Jesus' disciples (the servants) and the Jewish leadership (the rebels). Concerning the latter, especially the scribes and Pharisees, Jesus spoke harshly at times. Read an example of this in Matthew 23. When you have finished reading, answer the following questions.

What evidence can you point to in Matthew 23 that indicates the scribes and Pharisees flaunted their leadership and had a lot of self-righteous pride?

In contrast, how did Jesus define greatness? (Matthew 23:11)

What quality did Jesus want his followers and leaders to manifest? (v. 12)

Why did the Jewish leadership not acknowledge Jesus as their Messiah and Savior? (v. 37)

Like the rebellious citizenry in the parable, when will the scribes and Pharisees see Jesus again? (v. 39)

Clearly, the scribes and Pharisees lacked a spiritual quality that would have made them teachable and able to hear and respond to Jesus in faith. This is not an uncommon problem. The Bible not only identifies this problem, but reveals the antidote as well.

The Spiritual Principle Identified

Open your Bible to Luke 5:1-8. Follow the progress of the interaction between Peter and Jesus by answering the questions below. The fisherman, Simon Peter, before he became a disciple of Jesus, illustrates an important spiritual principle relevant to the problem above.

Peter was a professional fisherman on the Sea of Galilee at the time of Jesus. He and his crew had completed a discouraging night of fishing and were cleaning their nets to wait for another day. Jesus was teaching in the area and told Peter to take the nets and go out fishing again.

What evidence do you find in this text that Peter was skeptical of any possible fishing success?

What title did Peter use to address Jesus, and how does this reflect Peter's limited understanding at this time of who Jesus really is (v.5)?

If asked at that time, how do you think Peter would compare his fishing skills and experience with those of Jesus?

Read the first two paragraphs on page 107 in SBF. Do you think the evaluation of Peter there as the "pro" is justified? Briefly defend your answer.

After catching two boat loads of fish on the first throw of the net, what title did Peter use to address Jesus (v.8)?

At that point what was Peter's attitude and evaluation of himself?

The important aspect of this incident is how Peter's view of both himself and Jesus changed along his path to faith. Complete the blanks below which summarize what happened (see the diagram on page 107 of SBF):

Peter changed from having [1] _____ to having [2] _____ and (in Peter's understanding) Jesus was no longer just a [3] _____ teacher but was [4] _____. This change in Peter's conviction was the result of "spiritual brokenness" in his heart. This principle is often the antidote for pride.

[5] _____ is what keeps many people from faith in Jesus Christ. A refusal to say "I'm sorry" to God about our sins and a reluctance to renounce our independent self-sufficiency can keep us from knowing God. Pride is also the chief cause of misery and alienation in the world. In order to get a more complete understanding of God's view of pride and humility, identify what the Bible teaches in each of the following Bible passages.

God's view of pride and humility:

What does God hate? (Proverbs 8:13)

What does God require? (Micah 6:8)

What does God oppose? (James 4:6) PROUD

Who receives God's grace? (James 4:6) humble

What is from the world and not from God? (1 John 2:16)

Jesus' example and teaching:

What is characteristic of Jesus' heart? (Matthew 11:29)

What example did Jesus give us that we are commanded to follow? (Philippians 2:5-8)

What did Jesus include in the list of evil things that come from within us? (Mark 7:21-23)

Application to Jesus' followers:

What characteristic should the servant of the Lord manifest? (Matthew 20:25-28)

I Am Second . com

What is commanded in our relations with others? (Philippians 2:3)

What characteristic is included for those who are the children of God? (Colossians 3:12)

What happens to us if we nurture pride in our life? (Proverbs 16:18)

Think of yourself, or others you have observed or heard about who are examples of wrongful pride. Circle as many words in the list below that you feel often fit the person or persons who manifested this pride.

Teachable	Divisive	Loving	Forgiving	Arrogant
Sensitive	Jealous	Tolerant	Angry	Patient
Generous	Kind	Competitive	Dissentious	Gentle

Compare the words you have circled with the two contrasting lists found in Galatians 5:19-23: the deeds of the flesh and the fruit of the Holy Spirit. In which list do you find more of the words you circled above?

Are there a lot of words from the fruit of the Spirit list that are not circled?

Based on this observation and what you have learned in this chapter, do you think pride should be thought of as a mere character flaw or a spiritual matter? Defend your answer.

> **"Pride leads to every other vice: it is the complete anti-God state of mind."**
> –C.S. Lewis, *Mere Christianity*, p. 109

[6] True/False. The "bottom line" in our willingness to acknowledge Jesus as our Savior and God is admitting and renouncing our pride, self-righteousness, and independent self-sufficiency.

The Spiritual Principle Illustrated

John the Baptist was a man empowered and used by God in a very significant way. What was the history of his personal development? Why was he pleasing to God? The Bible makes it clear that he manifested the principle of spiritual brokenness which we identified in this chapter. Find out for yourself as you complete the blanks and answer the questions below.

John the Baptist

John was born into a [7] _____ or Levite family (Luke 1:5). The priests were Sadducees, often wealthy Aristocrats and were influential in Jesus' time.

Incredible things were said by the angel [8] _____ (Luke 1:19) about how important John would be (Luke 1:15-17). He would also be the first prophet in Israel for 400 years.

What evidence is there in Matthew 3:5-6 and Luke 3:10-14 that John's ministry was impacting a lot of people from many walks of life?

In their excitement and state of expectancy, the people were thinking that John the Baptist may have been the Christ (Messiah). That could have been a temptation to John to bask in the attention. Instead, what attitude did he manifest in what he said? (Luke 3:16)

John's exploding ministry was only about six months old when Jesus began His ministry. When Jesus came to John and asked to be baptized by him, what attitude did John manifest in what he said? (Matthew 3:13-14)

About the same time, John's disciples expressed some jealousy since many people were going to Jesus rather than coming to John (John 3:22-30). Note John's response by answering the questions below.

Where did John say his ministry and success came from? (v. 27)

What does John understand and accept his role to be? (v. 28)

What does John say his relationship to Jesus is? (v. 29)

What gives him joy? (v. 29)

John's crowning words were: "He must [9] _____, but I must [10] _____" (v. 30). What a great example of spiritual brokenness, just as is illustrated in the rectangle diagram! (SBF, p. 107) Like Peter along the path to faith, while John the Baptist's upper triangle was getting smaller (left to right), Jesus' triangle was getting larger. The same should be true if we put our name in the upper triangle.

How did Jesus describe John the Baptist? (Luke 7:26-28)

"...one who is [11] _____ than a prophet."

"I say to you, among those born of women, there is no one [12] _____ than John..."

What a wonderful epitaph for John the Baptist—a life characterized by humility.

Two Key Questions

Moses

Moses was another man whom God used in a profound way. Interestingly, his life is divided into three, forty-year periods, as described below. Fill in the blanks by referring to the Bible passages cited.

First Forty – Moses was a man of great status, having been raised in the palace of Egypt as the adopted son of the Pharaoh. He is described in Acts 7:22 as "educated in all the learning of the Egyptians, and he was a man of (13) _____ in words and deeds." Because of his position and power, he mistakenly took vengeance into his own hands by killing an Egyptian and appointed himself as (14) _____ of the Israeli slaves (Acts 7:23-25).

Second Forty – Moses wandered in the desert as a hunted man, a nomad because of his murder of the Egyptian (Acts 7:28-29). The most educated and capable Jew in the world was working for his father-in-law, shepherding animals! But this experience remedied his extreme case of self-sufficiency. The "pro" had failed, so to speak. It was his time of (15) _____.

Third Forty – Moses was used by God to deliver the people of Israel from their slavery in Egypt (Exodus 3). In fact, his reputation as a man of God is based entirely on this final third of his life, after he had reached the age of (16) _____! (Exodus 7:7). He died at 120 years of age (Deuteronomy 34:7).

Read SBF, pages 109-112, to become more acquainted with the details of Moses' life and the author's commentary. Even though Moses was undoubtedly the most educated and powerful Jew in the world of his time, he had to experience his own brokenness before God used him.

What Moses needed to understand can be identified with two questions he asked at the burning bush incident. The first is "Who am (17) _____?" (Exodus 3:11), or "Who do I think I am?"

What do you think is the significance of God's statement (v. 12) that "Certainly I will be with you…"?

The second question is, "God, who are (18) _____?" (Exodus 3:13).

What do you think is the significance of God's answer to Moses' question as recorded in Exodus 3:14?

How is God's action, as recorded in Exodus 4:1-8, relevant to Moses' second question?

Contrast the difference in Moses' attitude: from perceiving himself to be the "deliverer" at the end of his first forty years (Acts 7:23-26) to his actually being used to deliver Israel in his third forty years (Exodus 3:11; 4:1, 10, 13). How do you explain this change in Moses?

If we apply the rectangle "path to faith" diagram to Moses' life, we could conclude that in his first forty years he was the [19] _____, and in his second forty years he learned [20] _____. He was then in position to be used greatly by God in his third forty years.

What did God think of Moses? Compare the two different descriptions of Moses found in Deuteronomy 34:10-12 and Numbers 12:3. Based on what you have learned in this chapter, how do you reconcile these two paradoxical descriptions?

Based on the brief study of John the Baptist in this chapter, write how you think John would have responded to the two questions: "Who am I?" and "God, who are you?"

[21] True/False. The author of the text, *Surprised by Faith*, also experienced brokenness which resulted in humility and a confession of Jesus as God (SBF, p. 117).

[22] True/False. One question each must ask himself/herself on the path to faith is, "Why am I so good?"

Some people may object to this concept of spiritual brokenness and confession of sin because they say it destroys the important need we have for self-esteem and personal worth. Use the discussion below to help you in preparing an answer to this objection.

> **"In God you come up against something which is in every respect immeasurably superior to yourself. Unless you know God as that—and, therefore, know yourself as nothing in comparison—you do not know God at all. As long as you are proud you cannot know God."**
>
> **—C.S. Lewis,** *Mere Christianity*, **p. 111**

God does not demean us nor ask us to grovel. His intention is to restore us to the potential He created us for. If everything about us and the world was wonderful and pure, we could perhaps question why brokenness and confession of sin are needed. But there is hostility, loneliness, emptiness, disillusionment, alienation and pain—all around us.

The Bible says these are the result of a flaw within humans called a sin nature (Galatians 5:19-21) which has caused us to go our own, self-centered way. God has the power and desire to fix us, but it requires radical surgery of the human heart. He promises that the Holy Spirit implanted within us (John 7:38-39; 1 Corinthians 6:19) will result in love, joy, peace, patience, kindness, goodness, faithfulness, gentleness and self-control (Galatians 5:22-23).

Years ago, when one of my sons was quite young, he was exercising his independence in belligerent and destructive ways. He was sure that he knew better than I, and that I desired a terrible thing for him. Tenseness, hostility and rejection prevailed. Finally, I responded with some discipline and correction. To my surprise, instead of driving him further from me, the discipline softened his heart to confess that he was sorry, and we embraced as we both shed some tears. It was healing—anger was turned to joy and the relationship was restored. Shortly afterward he was cheerful as if a very large "load" had been lifted from his young life.

Likewise, our self-esteem and personal worth are set free to soar when the bondage we have to sin and pride is broken. If the Son sets you free, you are truly free to be all you were intended to be (John 8:36). It is a positive life change.

(23) True/False. The pride of refusing to admit we are all sinners in need of a Savior is the greatest deterrent to faith in Christ.

(24) True/False. A person's spiritual humility and submission to God are keys to being used by Him in life and ministry.

Spiritual brokenness is often experienced on our path to faith. Spiritual brokenness is the change in one's personal perception from a self-sufficient and conceited "pro" to a dependant "sinner" repentant before God; a change in attitude and conviction which results from the work of God's Spirit. It is the antidote to the pride which separates us from a holy God. That's our ninth *FaithSearch* discovery.

Ah-ha!
The DISCOVERY

Pride keeps more people from faith and forgiveness in Jesus Christ than any other factor!

Application and Reflection

Two key questions were identified in this session: "Who am I?" and "God, who are You?" Do you agree that these are important questions which people must ask and honestly answer along the path to faith?

Have these questions been a factor in your own path to faith? Write briefly about your own experience.

Ah-ha!

| Discovery #9 |
| Stumbling Block: Pride |

| Discovery #8 |
| New Relationship, Freedom, Hope |

| Discovery #7 |
| Certain Object, Valid Faith |

| Discovery #6 |
| Jesus Backed His Claim |

| Discovery #5 |
| Jesus Claimed to be God |

| Discovery #4 |
| Historically Reliable Records |

| Discovery #3 |
| Eyewitness Records |

| Discovery #2 |
| God Became Flesh |

| Discovery #1 |
| No God? DEATH Wins |

In telling others about your faith, have you found some for whom a confession of faith in Jesus Christ is difficult?

If so, what percentage of them do you think had pride as a stumbling block to faith?

What other reasons do you think keep people from making a confession of faith and following Jesus?

One of the common objections by unbelievers to becoming a Christian is the problem of evil. The problem, stated simply, is, "How can the Christian God—who, according to the Bible, is all-powerful and all-good—allow evil to triumph in such events as the Holocaust and the World Trade Center Towers?" Use the following discussion to help you in formulating an answer.

The Holocaust and the attack on the World Trade Center are just two of many atrocities which have been witnessed in history. Car accidents, murder, AIDS and genocide, all can be found by scanning one day's news. "Why?" is the most-frequently asked question. In fact, when the pollster George Barna asked Americans, "If you could ask God one question and knew He would give you an answer, what would you ask?"—the top response (17%) was, "Why is there so much pain and suffering?" The answer to this question is found at two levels of human experience.

The first level is the intellectual. C.S. Lewis expressed the underlying logic in this area: "If God were good, He would wish to make His creatures perfectly happy, and if God were almighty, He would be able to do what He wished. But the creatures are not happy. Therefore God lacks either goodness, or power, or both" (*The Problem of Pain* [New York: Macmillan, 1962], p. 26). Some go even further than Lewis to suggest that the Christian God does not exist at all, and cite all the evil in the world as evidence.

The answer to this difficult question is found in the subject of human free will. The fact that God is all-powerful does not mean He can do anything, particularly things that would be a self-contradiction. For example, God cannot create colorless color or a round square. Likewise, God cannot create people to have genuine freedom and yet have no potential for sin—of choosing evil. Creating people with free will opens the door to the overwhelming majority of pain in the world—people choosing evil over God.

Could God have created a world without human freedom? Yes, if He had stopped after the animals and plants there would have been no hate or suffering. But the ultimate value in the universe would also be missing—love. Without choice there can be no love. God knows that the value of love in both the temporal and eternal realms far exceeds the downside of suffering for a time. C.S. Lewis referred to pain as the megaphone of God. He meant that it is often the way God gets our attention, awakens us out of our stupor of independence from Him, and calls us into relationship with Him. Besides, for those who love God, He promises that He is bringing good into our lives, such as character development, even in the midst of our suffering (Romans 8:28). The bottom line here is that God's perspective for us is eternal, "not wishing for any to perish but for all to come to repentance" (2 Peter 3:9).

The second level of the problem of evil is personal. We suffer, and we want to know whether God cares. Yes, He said that He loves us so much that He came Himself to die on the cross so we can have a new quality of life here and forever (John 3:16). We suffer, and we want to know whether God understands. Yes, He said that He has experienced all our pain and temptation as well, so that He desires to provide grace and mercy in our time of need (Hebrews 4:15-16). We suffer, and we want to feel His touch and silent, comforting presence. Yes, He promised never to leave or forsake us (Deuteronomy 31:6) and that He would give rest to all who are weary and heavy-laden (Matthew 11:28-29).

Finally, we wonder if there is an ultimate solution to pain and suffering. Yes, Jesus said the day is coming when those who believe in Him will be placed on a new heaven and earth where "there will no longer be any death; there will no longer be any mourning, or crying, or pain…" (Revelation 21:4).

Therefore, though everything around us may not be making sense and there are still unanswered questions, we have to ask honestly whether anyone besides Christians has an answer to the problem of evil at all, much less an answer with such a wonderful future and hope.

Confirming the Discovery

Read the references below in a Bible, or as provided here in the margin. Write after each one how the main teaching of each passage relates to or confirms the discovery made in this chapter.

Romans 3:9-10, 22-23

Proverbs 8:13

Micah 6:8

Proverbs 16:18

2 Chronicles 7:14

In summary of God's Word, both the Old and New Testaments teach the doctrine of universal sin which has separated the entire human race from a relationship with their holy God (Psalm 14:1-3; Romans 3:9, 22-23). Often sin is manifested as pride and independence from God, which God calls evil and which God hates (Proverbs 8:13). In contrast, God calls humility good and says that it pleases Him when we walk humbly with Him (Micah 6:8).

For more details on this subject see:
Lee Strobel, *The Case for Faith* (Grand Rapids: Zondervan, 2000), pp. 25-55.

Philip Yancey, *Where Is God When It Hurts* (Grand Rapids: Zondervan, 1990).

…for we have already charged that both Jews and Greeks are all under sin; as it is written, "There is none righteous, not even one"…for there is no distinction; for all have sinned and fall short of the glory of God…
—**Romans 3:9-10, 22-23**

"The fear of the Lord is to hate evil; Pride and arrogance and the evil way, And the perverted mouth, I hate."
—**Proverbs 8:13**

He has told you, O man, what is good; And what does the Lord require of you but to do justice, to love kindness, And to walk humbly with your God?
—**Micah 6:8**

Pride goes before destruction, and a haughty spirit before stumbling.
—**Proverbs 16:18**

"…and [if] my people who are called by My name humble themselves and pray and seek My face and turn from their wicked ways, then I will hear from heaven, will forgive their sin, and will heal their land."
—**2 Chronicles 7:14**

Pride makes us blind to the ways of God and leads to a life of moral error and eternal destruction in the end (Proverbs 16:18). On the other hand, God promises that if in humbleness we seek Him and forsake sin, he will hear us, forgive us and restore what sin had destroyed (2 Chronicles 7:14).

Looking Ahead

As you review the diagram on page 101 in SBF, how have you answered the question at the top? If you are below the line in unbelief or doubt and have not said to God, "I'm sorry for my sin," and trusted Jesus as your Savior, search your heart to honestly determine if pride might be the reason. In the next chapter, an opportunity will be provided to say "yes" and to take the next step of crossing over the line to faith.

Answers for the objective questions in this chapter:

1. pride	2. humility	3. human	4. God	5. Pride
6. True	7. priestly	8. Gabriel	9. increase	10. decrease
11. more	12. greater	13. power	14. deliverer	15. brokenness
16. eighty	17. I	18. you	19. pro	20. humility
21. True	22. False	23. True	24. True	

CHAPTER 10

Discovering the *"Ah-Ha!"* of Life
Taking the First Step of a Faith Commitment to Follow Jesus

Getting FOCUSED

- How can becoming a Christian be both hard and easy at the same time?
- What do people mean when they say they know God personally?
- Is there one God or three?

Becoming a Christian and knowing God is easy because it's a free gift—offered by God through His grace. Discovering the *"Ah-Ha!"* of life is only a prayer away. In confession, on our knees at the foot of the cross of Jesus, we receive God's gift of forgiveness, are created with new life by God the Holy Spirit, and adopted as spiritual children into His family. The transformation that results is fulfilling and deeply meaningful in our life now—and assures us of living in heaven with God for eternity. People of every race, nationality, gender, age, status in life, culture and geographic region all testify to its reality in their experience.

Making the DISCOVERY

The text of **FaithSearch** Discovery, *Surprised by Faith* (pp. 101-104; 117-121) will help you to answer the questions and make the discovery in this chapter.

Introduction

In chapter 6 we realized that a choice—acceptance or rejection of Jesus—was the basic issue of faith. For those who have already come down the path of new life in Jesus Christ, you will find in this chapter confirmation of "the way" and hopefully sharpen your skills to give better directions for the road map of life discovery to others.

This chapter is primarily for anyone who is outside of the Christian faith looking in, who isn't sure whether they are out or in, or who wants to make sure. In other words, it is information and an invitation to an honest person who wants to know what the next step is. As you will see, that step is not difficult to understand.

First, though, you may have wondered if there is any proof of the reality of life after death. Read the discussion below to give you additional perspective on this important question. Write a brief answer of your own in which you identify which argument is the most convincing to you.

A Leader's Guide is available with answers to these questions, guidelines for leading small group interaction, and other helpful resources. It's available free by downloading it from the **FaithSearch** Web site (www.faithsearch.org). For a small fee plus postage, a printed copy can be requested from the **FaithSearch** office (952-401-4501).

It is important to recognize that having a longing for life after death is a good thing. C.S. Lewis once wrote:

> ...a continual looking forward to the eternal world is not (as some modern people think) a form of escapism or wishful thinking, but one of the things a Christian is meant to do. It does not mean that we are to leave the present world as it is. If you read history you will find that the Christians who did most for the present world were just those who thought most of the next (*Mere Christianity*, [New York: Macmillan, 1952], p. 118).

A Gallup poll taken in 1994 revealed that 71% of people in the United States believe there is life after death. What evidence is there for this? There are four lines of evidence, three circumstantial and one direct. First, medical studies of the relation between body and spirit, primarily by studying near death experiences (NDEs), suggest there is more to people than just the physical. Conscious memory seems to exist even when machines indicate flat brain waves and no heart rhythm. Second, physiological studies on the brain itself have revealed that there seems to be a separate identity and existence apart from the body. We are more than the sum total of our cells and anatomical structure. The third circumstantial evidence has to do with unsatisfied longings or unfulfilled desires. C.S. Lewis wrote, "If I find in myself a desire which no experience in this world can satisfy, the most probable explanation is that I was made for another world" (*Mere Christianity*, pp. 119-120). This may explain the meaningfulness of certain themes of Scripture, for example, Psalm 23, John 10, and Revelation 7 and 21:1-5.

The only direct evidence that there is life after death is that a real person in human history demonstrated it to be true! The bodily resurrection of Jesus Christ–supported by the facts of His empty tomb, of at least ten post-resurrection appearances, of eyewitness testimony, and of the transformed lives of His disciples–is the basis for certainty about life after death. Jesus died and then spent forty days physically on earth after he rose from the dead, appearing at one point to more than 500 people simultaneously (1 Corinthians 15:5-8). He said, "I am the resurrection and the life; he who believes in Me will live even if he dies…" (John 11:25). Jesus' promise to His followers is that He is preparing a place for each one in heaven, saying also, "I will come again, and receive you to Myself; that where I am, there you may be also" (John 14:2-3).

For more information about the evidence for the resurrection of Jesus see pages 65-69 in SBF, and William Lane Craig, *The Son Rises* (Chicago: Moody, 1981). For details about life after death see Gary Habermas, *Beyond Death* (Crossway Books, 1998).

Where Am I?

Because of widespread belief in the existence of God, people who hold that conviction may feel they are okay spiritually. They may wonder why there is a need for faith in Jesus as well. Their position is: "I already believe [in God]." Is believing in God–or that God exists–really enough? Is it the same as personal faith in Jesus? Formulate your own answer for someone who takes that position. Use the discussion below for assistance.

Polls in the United States consistently reveal that about 95% of us believe in the existence of God or a higher power. Does this mean that 95% of Americans are in right relationship with God? Not according to Jesus. He said that no one can come to the Father except through Him (John 14:6). His own, personally-trained disciples stated that a right relationship with

God (salvation) is found only through Jesus (Acts 4:12). For an explanation of the reason for this, see "Aren't Good People Good Enough?" on page 75.

As recorded in John 8:34-47, Jesus was interacting with some Jewish leaders. Jesus stated that anyone who sins is a slave to sin (v. 34), but that He as the Son of Man can set us free (v. 36). The Jewish leaders denied being in bondage to sin and declared their belief in God (v. 41). Jesus said that if they were truly of God they would love Him (v. 42). But their rejection of Him means they are children of the devil and do not belong to God (vv. 44, 47). The conclusion to Jesus' teaching here is this: If I won't confess faith in Jesus as God the Son, then I don't have a right relationship with God the Father either. Why?

The entire human race was in despair until God announced that He would be our redeemer (Isaiah 43:1). This is the genius of the incarnation of Jesus Christ to earth. Because Jesus Christ is God, He is holy and without sin. Because He is human, he is qualified to represent us as our redeemer. No other human has ever been holy and able to offer Himself to God as our substitute and as a just ransom to redeem us from sin and death. As the apostle Peter said, "For Christ also died for sins once for all, the just for the unjust, so that He might bring us to God" (1 Peter 3:18). That's why Jesus, without being intolerant, can say, "I am the way and the truth and the life. No one comes to the Father but through me" (John 14:6). It's a true statement!

Jesus becomes our way to God when we enter into personal faith in Him, as the apostle John states: "Yet to all who received Him [Jesus], to those who believed in His name, He gave the right to become children of God…" (John 1:12, NIV). Merely "believing in God" will not take away our sin, nor will it save us, nor will it admit us to heaven when we die. After all, James reminds us that even the demons believe God is one (James 2:19), yet their intellectual assent has not made them children of God. The apostle John makes the way definitively clear: "And the testimony is this, that God has given us eternal life, and this life is in His Son. He who has the Son has the life; he who does not have the Son of God does not have the life" (1 John 5:11-12).

The diagram on the next page identifies the various positions each person may be in relative to the question, "Have I placed my faith in Jesus Christ alone for my salvation?" Review the reasons that someone may say "no" to Jesus by completing the blanks below (SBF, pp. 101-102).

The Unbelief Positions ("No")

Lack of [1] _____ of Jesus Christ (ignorant unbelief)

[2] _____ about Jesus Christ (doubt)

Willful [3] _____ of Jesus Christ (decisional unbelief)

As you reflect on your life, have you ever been at one of these positions? If so, describe how you felt at that time, and whether or how you came out of it.

Do any of these positions describe where you are right now? If so, identify which one, tell how you feel and explain your reasons for being in that position.

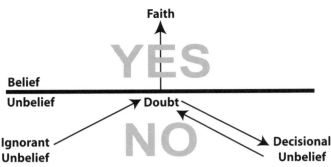

Are you willing to seek help to change your position from a "no" to a "yes" regarding Jesus Christ? If so, read about the antidote to these positions in SBF (pp. 94-96) and see the suggestions in the "Looking Ahead" section at the end of this chapter.

The Belief Position ("Yes")

In chapter 9 we discovered why a "yes" to Jesus may be hard for some: their self-sufficiency and pride keep them from acknowledging their sin and submitting to the cross of Jesus for forgiveness and new life. But even if that is not a problem for you, there may still be a misconception about what a "yes" response to Jesus means. Read the section, "The Operation of Belief" (SBF, pp. 96-99), and match all the words on the right with the appropriate "faith" on the left.

(4) _____ Genuine Faith

a. Contract   f. Disappointment

b. Surrender   g. Unconditional

c. Conditions   h. Personal Fulfillment

d. God's terms   i. "I believe God, period"

e. "I'll believe if…"

(5) _____ Counterfeit Faith

Take time to reflect honestly about your faith in Jesus Christ (or anticipated faith). Is there any sort of a "deal" with God in your heart? List any conditions or expectations you have of God.

If there are some things you expect God to do or provide for you (i.e. making a contract or a deal), do you see how you could be tempted to doubt God's faithfulness if you don't get what you expect? Has that ever happened to you? Explain.

Explain how the Bible passages of Matthew 22:37 and Hebrews 12:2a help to direct your focus toward having genuine faith in God without conditions.

What difference does Jesus make in my life?

We have just concluded that genuine faith is focused on God, not on rewards or benefits which may come to us as a result. But if a confession of faith in Jesus Christ sets us free from our bondage to sin, and the Holy Spirit creates us anew and lives within us, then we really should expect to experience some differences in our life. Read page 103 in SBF and identify in your own words the differences you can expect Jesus to make in your life when you confess faith in Him.

Millions of people share their testimony of a changed life as a result of personal faith in Jesus Christ. But some may still say that religious experience is so subjective that it doesn't prove anything. How would you answer them? Read the discussion below for assistance in formulating your response.

> **"Following Jesus Christ has been an experience of increasing challenge, adventure and happiness. He is totally worthwhile. How true are His words: 'I am come that they might have life, and that they might have it more abundantly.'"**
>
> **–Testimony of Mark Hatfield, former U.S. Senator from Oregon**

There is a chorus of people who claim to have found joy, tranquility and a host of other benefits—attributing their life change to a variety of sources or activities. Are any of these claims valid? How can we know? It is true that our experiences are considered anecdotal or "soft" evidence. But is it so subjective that it doesn't prove anything? Consider the following illustration from Josh McDowell, as discussed in *Evidence that Demands a Verdict* (San Bernardino: Here's Life, 1979), p. 327-328:

> For example, let's say a student comes into the room and says, "Guys, I have a stewed tomato in my right tennis shoe. This tomato has changed my life. It has given me a peace and love and joy that I never experienced before"…It is hard to argue with a student like that if his life backs up what he says…A personal testimony is often a subjective argument for the reality of something…There are two questions or tests I apply to a subjective experience. First, what is the objective reality for the subjective experience, and second, how many other people have had the same subjective experience from being related to the objective reality?

When asked how he accounts for his life change, the student would answer, "A stewed tomato in my right tennis shoe." But to find even one other person in the entire world who has had a similar life change as a result of a stewed tomato in their right tennis shoe is improbable. The objective reality is more than a little suspect when it cannot be verified repeatedly in the lives of others.

On the other hand, when a Christian is asked for the objective reality that has resulted in a significant subjective life change, he/she would answer, "The person of Christ and His resurrection." How many others share this same result from a relationship with Jesus Christ? The evidence is overwhelming. There are millions of people from every nationality and profession who have experienced this kind of positive life change. As William Wilson, a former dean of clinical neurophysiology exclaims (*Decision* magazine, October 1977):

> Doing research in Christian experiences, I was impressed with what conversion achieved. In fact, I was astounded. Drunkards were turned into sober people; heroin addicts into nonusers; depressed people into well-regulated people; angry people into gentle, kind people; fearful people into brave people; self-centered, prideful people into humble, loving people.

Such broad confirmation greatly increases the validity of the life-changing claim of faith in Jesus.

A Personal Invitation

To summarize some of the points you have learned in this chapter, complete the blanks below.

God [6] _____ the world by his infinite wisdom and power (Intelligent Design).

Two thousand years ago God became [7] _____ in the person of Jesus Christ and lived in the world that He created.

Jesus Christ died on the cross as my [8] _____ (taking the death I deserved).

Jesus Christ's death redeemed me from [9] _____ and [10] _____ from God.

Jesus Christ broke the power of death by His [11] _____ from the grave.

I am saved and enter into a personal relationship with God upon [12] _____ with my mouth that Jesus is Lord and [13] _____ in my heart that He was resurrected from the dead (Romans 10:9).

In taking this step to know God, I confess that Jesus Christ is

    a) My [14] _____ (Colossians 1:16)

    b) My [15] _____ (Ephesians 1:7)

    c) My [16] _____ _____ (1 Peter 1:3)

(17) True/False. The Bible teaches that we can know with certainty whether we are going to heaven when we die (1 John 5:11-13).

What is God's will for us? Has God told us what He desires for us? Read the two Bible passages referenced below and write down specifically what He says.

2 Peter 3:9

1 Timothy 2:3-4

At a sensitive time in Jesus' ministry He was deeply moved. He was giving a tribute to John the Baptist (Matthew 11:7ff) and then He was burdened by the hardness and lack of repentance in some of the cities of Israel (vv. 20-24). He then turned to His Father in prayer and praise that the teachable and the humble were indeed coming to Him in repentance and faith (vv. 25-26). It was in this context that He gave His own invitation and promise to all who would come to Him as their Savior and Lord:

> "Come to Me, all who are weary and heavy-laden, and I will give you rest. Take My yoke upon you, and learn from Me, for I am gentle and humble in heart, and you will find rest for your souls. For My yoke is easy, and My burden is light" (Matthew 11:28-30).

Jesus' invitation is to discover the *"Ah-Ha!"* of life. That is our tenth **FaithSearch** discovery.

Ah-ha!
The DISCOVERY

I can experience a vital relationship with God and the assurance of life after death by a confession of faith in Jesus Christ through prayer!

Application and Reflection

If you have not yet repented of your sin and confessed faith in Jesus Christ, are you willing to do so?

Ah-ha!

Discovery #10
A Miracle of New Life

Discovery #9
Stumbling Block: Pride

Discovery #8
New Relationship, Freedom, Hope

Discovery #7
Certain Object, Valid Faith

Discovery #6
Jesus Backed His Claim

Discovery #5
Jesus Claimed to be God

Discovery #4
Historically Reliable Records

Discovery #3
Eyewitness Records

Discovery #2
God Became Flesh

Discovery #1
No God? DEATH Wins

> "The most disappointing fact in my life, I believe, is that I waited so long before I discovered the fellowship of Jesus Christ. How much more wonderful my life would have been if I had taken this step many years earlier!"
>
> —Testimony of Tom Landry, former football coach of the NFL Dallas Cowboys

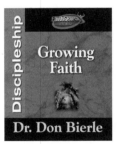

If yes, you may use the suggested prayer below as a guide for what to say:

> Dear God,
>
> Having discovered the truth about Jesus, I want to experience the miracle of new life which He came to give. I believe that Jesus is Lord, and that You raised Him from the dead. I confess my sin which has separated me from You, and now turn from it. Thank You for forgiving me, and for Your promise of eternal life in heaven with You when I die. I want to follow You in obedience through the guidance of Your Word. Amen.

If you prayed this prayer *for the first time,* congratulations! Read page 121 in SBF for information on taking the next step. I suggest that you use the card inside the back cover of SBF to record your confession and request a free copy of *Growing Faith*, a Bible study guide that will strengthen your faith, to help you experience the abundant life Jesus promised.

If you had *previously* made a personal confession of faith in Jesus Christ, explain below what brought you to that point and how it has changed your life. If it was a very recent commitment, explain how you *expect* it to make a future difference in your life.

Every believer should be nurtured in how to read and study the Bible and in the basic elements of the Christian life. This can be in a one-to-one relationship with a more mature Christian or in a small group discipleship class.

If you have not yet received such nurture, are you willing to take that next step to strengthen your faith? If you are, read page 121 in SBF and begin a personal or group study of *Growing Faith*. This Bible study will establish you in your faith to help you experience the abundant life Jesus promised. The *Growing Faith* material will also provide encouragement and guidance for getting involved in a local church. There you can experience support and community among believers, as well as help in growing in your Christian walk.

As a result of faith in Christ, our life is different in all the following ways, *except* one. Put a line through it: [18]

    a) We have peace with God
    b) We have certainty of eternal life
    c) We have concern about future judgment
    d) We are a child of God

At some time or another, nearly everyone seeks to understand more fully the concept of God as a Trinity. Some critics insist that Christians believe in three Gods instead of one. When does three equal one? Read the discussion below for insight into your own understanding and for greater capability of communicating to others what you believe.

The Christian concept of God as Trinity is based on God's own revelation of Himself in the Bible. It is not a man-made scheme or distortion. For example, we are instructed to baptize in the name (singular) of the Father, the Son and the Holy Spirit (Matthew 28:19). The Trinitarian benediction is given as the grace of the Lord Jesus Christ, the love of God, and the fellowship of the Holy Spirit (2 Corinthians 13:14). However, the Bible also affirms that God is "one" (Deuteronomy 6:4; Ephesians 4:6). How are we to understand this?

The "oneness" is in reference to God's being, substance or essence as "spirit" (John 4:24), rather than a "material" substance. As spirit, God is invisible (John 1:18; 1 Timothy 6:16) and personal, i.e., with intellect, will and emotion. In this divine spiritual essence God is infinite, omniscient, holy, just, omnipotent, etc. But the Bible's assertion of oneness teaches a multiplicity in unity. For example, the Bible's teaching that in marriage the two become _one_ flesh does not eliminate that there are still two persons. Jesus' prayer that His disciples would all be _one_ (John 17:21) does not mean they have ceased being separate persons. This is the meaning of multiplicity in unity.

The "threeness" of God—the Father is God (Galatians 1:1), the Son is God (John 1:1; 5:18) and the Holy Spirit is God (Acts 5:3-4)—is in reference to persons. There are three persons within the divine unity or spiritual essence. Thus, we do not have a contradiction unless we affirm the same thing at the same time in the same way. We affirm _one_ in regard to essence. We affirm _three_ in regard to persons. This may be difficult to comprehend, but it is not irrational or illogical.

Illustrations of the concept of trinity are never perfect, but sometimes help. Water is one chemical substance or essence (H_2O) but exists in three forms as solid (ice), liquid, and gas (steam). One family consists of father, mother and child. We are one being with body, soul and spirit. So, why not a God who is both one and a plurality in the Godhead? The Trinity is the most consistent view of God from all the strands of biblical data.

Confirming the Discovery

Read the references below in a Bible, or as provided here in the margin. Write after each one how the main teaching of each relates to or confirms the discovery made in this chapter.

Acts 4:12

Romans 8:1-2

Galatians 4:6-7

James 4:7-8, 10

John 6:40

For a more detailed discussion of this topic, see Robert Crossley, _The Trinity_ (Downers Grove: InterVarsity, 1965) and Robert Bowman, Jr., _Why You Should Believe in the Trinity_ (Grand Rapids: Baker, 1989).

"And there is salvation in no one else; for there is no other name under heaven that has been given among men, by which we must be saved."
—**Acts 4:12**

There is therefore now no condemnation for those who are in Christ Jesus. For the law of the Spirit of life in Christ Jesus has set you free from the law of sin and of death.
—**Romans 8:1-2**

Because you are sons, God has sent forth the Spirit of His Son into our hearts, crying, "Abba! Father!" Therefore, you are no longer a slave, but a son; and if a son, then an heir through God.
—**Galatians 4:6-7**

Submit therefore to God. Resist the devil and he will flee from you. Draw near to God and He will draw near to you....Humble yourselves in the presence of the Lord, and He will exalt you.
—**James 4:7-8, 10**

"For this is the will of My Father, that everyone who beholds the Son and believes in Him will have eternal life, and I Myself will raise him up on the last day."
—**John 6:40**

In summary of God's Word, the consistent testimony of Scripture is that salvation for all people is through Jesus alone. (Compare John 14:6, 1 Timothy 2:5 and 1 John 5:11-12.) As a result of our confession of faith in Jesus, we are redeemed from sin and eternal death and stand humbly before the throne of God without judgment (Romans 8:1-2). In Christ we have settled with God "out of court."

We also enjoy an incredible privilege to be spiritually adopted into the family of God because the Holy Spirit conceives new life within us. We are God's own adopted children and receive from Him our inheritance of eternal life (Galatians 4:6-7). To live our lives victoriously, we are commanded to submit, draw near, and humble ourselves before God. As a result the devil will flee from us, and God will draw near and exalt us (James 4:7-8,10).

Finally, Jesus clearly stated that God's will is for all to have eternal life through faith in His Son, and that He personally guarantees our resurrection (John 6:40).

Looking Ahead

If your answer to the question, "Have I placed my faith in Jesus Christ alone for my salvation?" is "Yes," take time to write out a brief testimony of your salvation that you could share with another person. The simple three-point outline below can be used as a structure for your testimony.

Before: Write a brief biographical sketch of your life before you became a Christian.

How: Describe the specific details of how you became a Christian.

After: Write a brief description of the changes which took place in your life.

If your answer to the question, "Have I placed my faith in Jesus Christ alone for my salvation?" is "No," use the space in the margin to explain why. Some resources are listed on pages 127-129 in SBF and a few more below. Perhaps they would help to answer questions you may still have. In addition, you are invited to call or write *FaithSearch* and ask to talk to someone. We would welcome an opportunity to help you in your quest for a personal faith in Jesus Christ.

FaithSearch International
105 Peavey Rd. STE 200
Chaska, MN 55318
USA
Phone: 952.401.4501
E-mail: info@faithsearch.org

Books and Booklets

Maiden, Brian. *One Way to God?* (London: InterVarsity Press, 1974).

Do all religions and sincere worshippers ultimately reach the same God? To suggest that any one faith is exclusively true is regarded today as intolerant and uncharitable. But the author gives solid reasons as he logically defends the position that Jesus Christ is the one way to God.

McDowell, Josh and Stewart, Don Douglas. *Answers to Tough Questions Skeptics Ask About the Christian Faith* (Nashville: T. Nelson Publishers, 1993).

Questions and brief answers about the Bible, God, miracles, Jesus Christ, world religions, creation, and faith. Strengthens the faith of the believer and helps to answer the inquiries of the skeptic regarding the credibility of Christianity.

Strobel, Lee. *The Case for Christ* (Grand Rapids, MI: Zondervan, 1998).

A journalist and former atheist with a law degree investigates the evidence for Jesus. He cross-examines a dozen experts who are recognized authorities in their own fields and have doctorates from schools like Cambridge, Princeton, and Brandeis. Highly readable and captivating.

Especially for Teens

Johnson, Kevin. *Can I Be a Christian Without Being Weird?* (Minneapolis, MN: Bethany House, 1992).

Readings for early teens on getting to know God. Relevant, highly readable, and life-changing.

Johnson, Kevin and White, James. *What's With the Mutant in the Microscope?* (Minneapolis, MN: Bethany House, 1999).

A look at the solid scientific reasons to believe God made the world. It examines the evidence (or lack of it) for evolution and intelligent design. An important topic, well written and with up-to-date facts.

Web Sites

1. The Discovery Institute. See www.discovery.org to get acquainted with scientific evidence for Intelligent Design in nature and the limited evidence for macroevolution.

2. Christian Research Institute. See www.equip.org for a depth and breadth of apologetic answers about Christianity, cults, etc.

3. Christian Answers Network. See www.christiananswers.net for a network of Christian ministries working together to provide answers to diverse issues and topics.

Answers for the objective questions in this chapter:

1. knowledge	2. Indecision	3. rejection	4. b, d, g, h, i
5. a, c, e, f	6. created	7. incarnate or flesh	8. substitute
9. sin	10. separation	11. resurrection	12. confession
13. believing	14. Creator	15. Redeemer	
16. resurrected Lord	17. True	18. c	

Events and Resources
from *FaithSearch* International

FaithSearch International exists to "Proclaim the Gospel with Evidence to All Peoples Everywhere." Our primary outreach and spiritual growth event for doing this is *FaithSearch* Discovery, for which *Surprised by Faith*—which you have just studied—is the supporting text. We encourage you to take advantage of this, and our other events and resources, as described below. They can help you grow in your faith; they can also help you share your discovery of faith with others.

Additional information is available on our Web site, including our events schedule (www.faithsearch.org). *FaithSearch* presenters are available to come to your church and community to conduct outreach and training events. You may contact *FaithSearch* by phone at 952.401.4501, (toll free at 800.964.1447) or by E-mail at info@faithsearch.org for information. (For your convenience you can order resources online.)

FaithSearch Discovery: Discovering the "Ah-ha!" of Life

FaithSearch Discovery presents an inspiringly logical case for believing in the historical person of Jesus Christ. Based on Dr. Bierle's book *Surprised by Faith*, this dynamic, live presentation is for everyone who wonders why they should believe—*and* for everyone who wonders why they do. The *FaithSearch* Discovery Participant Guide supports the presentation by providing thought-provoking questions and helpful review. (The *FaithSearch* Discovery PowerPoint® presentation—as used by *FaithSearch* evangelists—is scheduled to be available for purchase in 2007.) *FaithSearch* Discovery has challenged, inspired and wonderfully changed hundreds of thousands of people, providing satisfying answers to life's important questions.

**FaithSearch Discovery
Participant Guide**

- Why am I here?
- Is Jesus really God?
- Is the Bible true?
- Can faith be reasonable?
- How can I know God?

FaithSearch Origins: Making Sense of Creation & Evolution

Biologist Donald A. Bierle, Ph.D., uses current scientific evidence to unravel creation, evolution and the meaning of life. His emphasis on the powerful concept of intelligent design will unite rather than divide people on this controversial subject. Stimulating and challenging, the *FaithSearch* Origins presentation and text are ideal for students, teachers, pastors and parents.

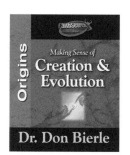

FaithSearch Origins text

FaithSearch Destiny: Making Sense of Life After Death

Using logic, and biblical and historical evidence, *FaithSearch* Destiny separates truth from fiction concerning the afterlife. This compelling presentation covers critical issues about the existence of God, the claims of reincarnation, the historical evidence for the resurrection of Jesus, fulfilled prophecy and the end of the world. *Making Sense of Life after Death* provides answers to questions each person should resolve about the course of life... and death.

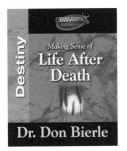

FaithSearch Destiny text

FaithSearch Influence: Friend to Friend

Friend to Friend is an exciting, positive outreach and discipleship training strategy that removes the "cookie-cutter" nature of some approaches. It empowers every Christian to become involved through relationships in his or her networks of influence. *Friend to Friend* presents the foundational principles for successful outreach and discipleship for the entire church, using *FaithSearch* events and resources. (The supporting PowerPoint presentation is scheduled to be released in 2007.)

FaithSearch Influence text

FaithSearch Discipleship: Growing Faith

The *FaithSearch* **Discipleship** workbook contains eight easy-to-follow lessons that help a person get firmly rooted in the truth of God's Word, the Bible. It is designed to be used for individual or group study, and in one-to-one discipleship. Each lesson is intellectually and spiritually challenging, leading the user through selected readings and key Scripture passages that help them understand what God *has* done and *will* do in their life. *Growing Faith* includes daily Bible readings and focus questions, as well as resources to expand and deepen your understanding of the Christian faith, on topics such as the Holy Spirit, overcoming doubt and temptation, learning to pray, and the importance of fellowship in the church. (Leader's Guide also available.)

FaithSearch Discipleship text

FaithSearch Video and Audio

Now *FaithSearch* presentations can be available any time, anywhere. Faithfully capturing our live presentations, these DVDs and audio CDs are ideal for use at home or church, in small or large group settings, for adults or youth, and for private study. A variety of topics is available, addressing timely issues with timeless answers. See our Web site (www.faithsearch.org) for the current list of titles and pricing.

FaithSearch DVDs and CDs